CRYSTAL WATERS

A GUIDE TO

HOT SPRINGS & THE OUACHITAS

Many individuals and agencies have contributed the
information used in this book. In limited instances,
grammatical corrections have been made, however it is
impossible to correct every error. Every attempt has been
made to preserve the "flavor" of the information presented,
but please be aware that the opinions expressed are those
of the individual writers.

CRYSTAL WATERS

A Guide To Hot Springs & The Ouachitas

By Dr. Pat Jordan

Heartland Press
Norman, AR

Published By Heartland Press
A Division of Heartland Crystal Institute
H.C. 67 Box 527 Norman, Ar 71960
(501) 867-3412

ISBN 0–9627113–0–6 $5.95

Cover Photo – Little Missouri Falls

Table of Contents

Crystal

1. A Short Study of Quartz — 2
2. Personalizing Your Crystal — 6
3. Crystal Digging — 10
4. Owning Your Own Mine — 19
5. Rockhounding In Arkansas — 21
6. Cleaning Crystals — 21
7. Quartz Festival — 25
8. Stanley's Fold — 26
9. Crystal Shops — 28
10. Vortex Areas in the Ouachitas — 30
11. Vortex Areas of Hot Springs — 34
12. Earth Changes in the Ouachitas — 36
13. Unified Energy Fields — 39
14. The Crystal Loop — 42
15. Little Missouri Falls — 44
16. Minerals in the Ouachitas — 47

Waters

17. Hot Springs — 48
18. Bathhouses — 51
19. Thermal Water Distribution — 53
20. Cold Springs — 54
21. History of Lake Ouachita — 55
22. Canoeing The Ouachita — 58
23. Canoeing-Profile of the River — 62
24. Types of Fish — 65
25. Fishing-Lake Ouachita — 66
26. Fishing-Lake Hamilton — 70
27. Water Sports — 77

28. Accommodations   80
29. Archaeology & Anthropology   90
30. Arts   100
31. Attractions   101
32. Boat Ramps   104
33. Camping   104
34. Cars:Street-Rods & Hot-Rods   106
35. Chambers of Commerce   108
36. Churches   108
37. Climate   108
38. Day Trips   109
39. Festivals & Fairs   112
40. Golf   114
41. Hiking   115
42. Hospitals   120
43. Hot Springs National Park   121
44. Hot Springs After Dark   124
45. Insects   124
46. Kids-Fun for the Younger Set   127
47. Lake Hamilton   129
48. Liquor   130
49. Lum'N'Abner   131
50. Maps   133
51. Mount Ida/Montgomery County   134
52. Newspapers   135
53. Oaklawn Racetrack   136
54. Ouachita Mountains   137
55. Physicians   138
56. Radio Stations   138
57. Restaurants   139
58. Retirement   143
59. Snakes   146
60. Television   149
61. Wildflowers   149

<u>**Acknowledgement**</u>

My heart felt thanks go first to David Johnson of Pencil Bluff. He has shared his history, his vision and his imagination. Without his spirit of adventure and his love of the Ouachitas this book would never have been created.

Jack Mc Pherson has been a mentor for every aspect of this book from the choice of computer to the final minute details. His wife, Jean, was an excellent proof reader. Without them, this book would not look the way it does.

Juanita Johnson served as proof reader and resident expert, Ginger Rickards as typist and friend and Joanna Parker who was willing to proof read in the twelfth hour. Debbie Baldwin and Betty Prince of the Montgomery County History Book have helped at a moments notice. Brian and Richard at Micro Computer have always been helpful.

My thanks go to my sister, Lynn, who has been supportive every step of the way with sweat as well as tears. Thank God no blood was ever shed! Speaking of God, I certainly didn't write this book alone, and have marveled throughout at the ease of this endeavor. My motto is, "I work with God, and God works with me." A Big Thanks.

Chris and Jody, my sons, are two special people who've been helpful in a multitude of ways and always patient.

I thank all those individuals who have contributed to this book by way of interviews and information. I never could have done this alone. I thank Dick Whittington, who was my first supporter. Thank–you to all the Mt. Ida residents who have helped make this book a reality.

Acknowlegements go to the following:
The U.S. Forest Service
The Army Corps of Engineers
The Hot Springs National Park
The Arkansas Dept. of Parks and Tourism
The Montgomery County Historical Society
The Chambers of Commerce of Mt. Ida & Hot Springs
The Arkansas Geological Commission
The Arkansas Fish & Game Commission
The Oklahoma Tourism & Recreation Department

___Introduction___

     Welcome to the Ouachita Mountains (pronounced Wash–i–taw). They are the best kept secret in Arkansas, perhaps the United States! The area is rich in history, natural wonders and scenic waters. It's a recreational paradise!

     Hot Springs has been ranked number three in the United States as a retirement location by Rand Mc Nally. Lake Ouachita is one of the cleanest and purest lakes in the country, and it is one of the finest tournament fishing lakes in the Northern Hemisphere.

     The area is geologically unique for two major reasons. For decades Hot Springs was an internationally known spa. As a place of healing thermal waters, it was sought by many for the theraputic characteristics of the 147 degree, bubbling spings. The "Valley of the Vapors" was revered by the Indians as a place of neutrality where any tribe could bathe without harm.

     Quartz crystal is the second geological feature of the area. The Ouachitas produce the largest amount of quartz crystal in the United States, and are famed for the size and types of crystal specimens they yield.

     In many respects, I am not the author of this volume. Perhaps, I am an editor, or more correctly a bridge. I have brought together information from many agencies and individuals with a diversity of backgrounds and ideas. I have included the flavor of the people. Sources are noted and no original material was changed. I encourage you to use this book as a springboard to seeks out your own areas of interest. My purpose is to offer information at the beginning of a trip that it might take two weeks or two years to learn.

     This book is dedicated to the people of the Ouachitas–both to the residents and to those visitors who will come and enrich our lives. Although I was born elsewhere, my heart lies in the Ouachitas.

CRYSTAL

1. A SHORT STUDY OF QUARTZ

By Duane Crandall & Ocus Stanley

Quartz is formed by the chemical union of the two most common elements:silicon and oxygen. The compound created by this union is silicon dioxide, and its various free forms compose almost 12 percent of the earth's outer shell. Silicon dioxide (quartz) has a glass-like luster, it breaks with a conchoidal fracture, and it has the hardness of 7 on Moh's scale which is 3 points under that of a diamond. It will scratch the hardest glass but cannot be scratched by the best steel knife blade. There are two main methods by which the crystallization of quartz may take place:
1. Solidification from a molten magna.
2. Precipitation of collodial silica out of a solution.

The second method is the most important and the most common. The nature of crystal deposits and their relation to other minerals which are destroyed at moderately high temperature are proof that quartz will crystallize at relatively low temperature and pressure. The rocks on the earth's surface and even at several feet deep are continually being broken down by weathering, erosion and chemical action. In this manner Silica is released. Water circulating down from the earth's surface picks up this Silica. The farther it travels through the earth the more Silica it carries until it reaches the saturation point. When this saturation point is reached, the water can carry no more Silica. As long as conditions remain stable. the water will pick up no more Silica nor will it deposit any of it. However, the slightest change in temperature or pressure or the entrance of some foreign material into the solution will cause it to become super-saturated, and it must deposit some of the Silica as a solid. If conditions are favorable, the Silica atoms will flow together in a symmetrical manner and form a hexagonal quartz crystal.

The crystals are usually deposited in cracks, crevices and pockets in the earth that have been caused by the cooling of the earth's surface, by faulting of the rocks and by shifting of the earth. The crystal thus formed will have a six- sided prism terminating in a six- sided pyramid. If conditions are stable and the solution is free from impurities, the Silica atoms will flow together slowly and smoothly. The prism of the crystal formed in this manner will be a perfect hexagon, and the six faces of the pyramid will be equal. However, since conditions are rarely perfect in nature, quartz crystals may be found in various shapes and sizes. The sides of the prism may be extremely unequal, and the terminating pyramid may have some large faces and others barely visible. Yet no matter what shape or form the crystal may be, the resultant angles between each face and their relationship to each other will be the same in each and every crystal.

Quartz crystals are the foundation on which the basic law of crystallography was established. (However much a crystal of any mineral may vary in size or shape, its corresponding interfacial angles are the same value, provided they are measured under the same condition.) In studying the prism of a quartz crystal we find that opposite faces are parallel and their interfacial angles are 120 degrees. The prism faces are rectangular in shape and their lateral edges form a right angle with the corresponding pyramid face. In measuring the angle between each pyramid face and its corresponding prism face, we find that the angle is almost 142 degrees, making the inclination of the pyramid face substantially 52 degrees.

Occasionally, in addition to the regular faces of the crystal there will occur an extra face, rhomboidal in shape, separating the prism face from the pyramid face. More rarely there will occur between this rhomboidal face and the prism face a trapezoidal face. When this trapezoidal face appears on the right side of the prism face, the crystal is called right-handed. When on the left side, it is called left-handed. Double terminating crystals, twins, phantoms, and crystals containing inclusions of foreign minerals are all sought by the collector because of their rarity.

Although many members of the quartz family are crystal-line, the three members that most readily form crystals are Rock Crystal, Amethyst, and Smoky Quartz. Rock Crystals are colorless and transparent and the finest quality have an ice-like appearance. The early Greeks thought the clear crystal was ice that had become so hard that it would no longer melt. They gave it the name 'Krustallos' from which the name crystal is derived.

Amethyst crystals have short prisms terminating in the usual pyramid. They range from violet to deep purple in color. Smoky Quartz crystals are in most ways similar to Rock Crystal except they have a smoky color ranging from faint smoke to almost black. The color is generally thought to be caused by exposure to some radioactive substance.

Ever since the very earliest times quartz crystals have been cut into jewelry and other works of lapidary art. Amethyst with its purple color was long a favorite of royalty. The fashionable ladies of ancient Rome carried small Rock Crystal spheres in their hands because of the refreshing coolness. And of course, even today, Rock Crystal balls are used by fortune-tellers and prophets to gaze into the future.

Quartz crystal has many commercial properties. The most important is its use in radio-transmitting and radar. A section of the crystal prism cut at a certain angle and a certain thickness will give off definite electrical oscillation. In this way, using sections cut at different angles and thicknesses, the wave lengths of radio stations can be controlled. Crystal quartz fused at a temperature of 1750 degrees is cast into lens blanks, rods, tubes, and sheets. The most notable of these is the 200 - inch telescope lens at Mount Palomar.

Quartz crystals have been found at many places scattered over the earth. Valuable deposits have been found in Brazil and on the island of Madagascar. In the U.S., Herkimer Co., NY is noted for small, brilliant crystals.

The Ouachita Mountain region of Montgomery and Garland Counties in Arkansas has long been noted for its fine quality crystal. In fact, when De Soto reached the Hot Springs valley, he found the local Indians doing a good business trading Rock Crystals to other tribes to be used for religious purposes. Mt. Ida, Montgomery Co., AR has been the center of extensive mining for nearly 100 years. In the strictest sense crystals are not mined; they are dug, a pick and shovel being the standard equipment. At times the digger can use nothing larger than an ice pick in extracting a delicate cluster or crystal burr.

Fisher Mt., seven miles east of Mt. Ida, is famous for gem-like Rock crystal. The crystals are found lining crevices between sandstone walls. At times these crevices open into large pockets. One such pocket yielded nearly 30 tons of fine quality single crystals, slabs, plates, and crystal burrs. To the north of Mt. Ida is a region of massive crystalline quartz called White Bluff. Here crystals are found in pockets buried within the rock. This massive rock has protected the crystals from much of the damage due to shifting of the earth's crust. To the south of Mt. Ida, many pockets have been found in the Collier Creek area. This area was the scene of extensive digging nearly 90 years ago. Although the Caddo Indians may have found crystal near the surface of the earth, now the digging of crystal calls for much hard but fascinating labor.

2. PERSONALIZING YOUR CRYSTAL

By Dr. Pat Jordan

Properties

Crystals are one of earth's most perfect creations. They range in color from perfectly clear optical quartz to milky white, yellowish citrine, smoky grey and violet amethyst. The color in no way makes one better than another. Just like people, their beauty is in variety. Crystals such as quartz form in molten lavas which are volcanically forced to the surface of the earth. Many are as old as the earth itself, others are still forming. The hardness of quartz on the Moh's scale is 7 and as such is a fairly hard material.

Quartz crystal is found throughout the United States. However, concentrated deposits occur in the Hot Springs area of Arkansas. Mexico and Brazil are foreign locations where large deposits of quartz are mined. The mining of crystals occurs in open rock piles or pits consisting of ribbons or layers of rock matrix, clay and quartz. Although crystals form in the clay, it is necessary to chip through the matrix to reveal them. You can mine crystals by hand with a pick, but extensive deposits must be exposed with larger equipment. In Arkansas you can see these crystal gems sparkling alongside many dirt roads. (See a following section on Mining Crystals.)

All quartz crystals have six sides parallel and end or terminate on at least one side in a point. Energy is said to travel along the sides in the direction of the point. If your crystal ends in a point on both ends, it is called "double terminated." In the case of double termination, energy may flow in both directions. Thus, the crystal can draw in energy as well as emit energy from both ends.

Uses

Crystals have many uses in the world of technology. They are used for memory storage as in computer chips, for frequency modulation as in radios, for transmitting energy from one location to another as in transistors, and for storing energy as in condensers. Just as crystals can be used technologically to transmit or send energy, amplify energy, receive energy and store energy, many people believe that crystals may function the same wOnay in their personal applications.

Quartz oscillates or vibrates at a precise rate. Many people experience the frequency or vibration rate of quartz to be helpful in keeping their "vibes" up or positive. In order to do this, keep your crystal around you, in your pocket or purse. For the greatest effect, hold your crystal in your left hand (unless you are left-handed, then use your right.)You may feel the energizing effects of the crystal flowing through your palm and around your body. However, it takes time to become sensitized to the subtle energies of crystal. A more focused exercise would be for you to sit comfortably with your crystal in your hand or hold it to your heart and spend ten minutes relaxing and re-energizing your body and emotions.

The memory function of the crystal may allow you to program or set a thought into your crystal. An example could be to amplify good thoughts and feelings and screen harmful ones. There is no judgement implied here. Your crystal and body know what is best for you! Try experimentation with your crystal. Move it around the outline of your body and see if you feel lighter or more energized. If you have an ache or pain, try moving the crystal 3 inches above the area and "pulling" the discomfort away. Use crystals in your plants; see if their growth changes. Keep one near your pet; watch for new energy levels.

Many cultures have believed in the properties of crystals throughout the ages. Whatever you believe or experience with crystals, it is important to remember that your attitude or <u>intention</u> is the most important ingredient in your use of a crystal. Approach the crystal only with thoughts that you would wish to have reflected or projected toward yourself. Think of it as a mirror that reflects the image you present to it. And like the volume dial on a radio, imagine it can amplify the frequency you have set it on.

Cleaning

Authors of books on crystals suggest cleansing your crystal when you acquire it. Different techniques on cleansing vary, but most recommend water and sunlight.(See section on Cleaning Crystals.) Submerging your crystal in salt water, either a mixture of sea salt and tap water or distilled water or ocean water from three hours to seven days is a common suggestion. Others feel that after the water cleanse, placing it in sunlight will help energize the crystal. For those who want a quick cleansing, draw a deep breath, imagine all energy but your own being removed from the crystal, and blow hard over the quartz. Some authors recommend burying the crystal in salt or dirt for a week to a month; however, this is a fairly drastic procedure. As you can see, there are many remedies for cleansing your crystal. In the end, the choice you make is personal.

Attuning your crystal to your vibrational frequency is believed by some to be important. This can be done by carrying the crystal with you, or sleeping with it under your pillow or keeping it on the nightstand. Again, the time required for this procedure varies from a day to a month, depending on the author.

Please don't throw up your hands in confusion! The most important suggestion that can be made in dealing with crystals is DO WHAT FEELS RIGHT FOR YOU! Let your own sense of the most appropriate process lead you. Crystals are tools or objects to be enjoyed, not items of ritual or worship. Like a mirror, they work best in the light and give you the clearest image when they are clean. And finally, the focus is not the crystal, but you–the most dazzling crystal of all.

3. CRYSTAL DIGGING

What do you imagine a crystal mine looks like? Many people visualize them as underground, dark and we—much like the tunnels in escape movies. They are exactly the opposite! Crystal mines in Arkansas, the largest producer of quartz in the United States, are open pit mines and look very much like strip mines. The pits appear barren and rocky except for bits of "sign" lying around. Sign may be milky quartz, clear quartz or various minerals often found with quartz. Red clay laced with matrix, the rock base from which the crystals grow, runs in veins on a northeast to southwest angle. These deposits may run for large distances along the vein, but you will often find little of the mineral to either side of the vein. As you enter a mine area, be sure to watch the ground for crystals sparkling at your feet. Seeing crystals is like looking for mushrooms. At first it is hard to distinguish them, and then suddenly you see them everywhere!

When To Go

Arkansas seasons are temperate, so you can dig comfortably most of the year, but in July and August temperatures can soar to the high nineties with high humidity. Remember, snakes like the same weather you do, and rattlers are sometimes found sunning on the rocks. During the summer, it is probably best to dig before eleven A.M. and after six P.M. Save the afternoons for swimming and water activities.

The winter months can be surprisingly mild. It is not unusual to have temperatures in the sixties on a sunny January day. However, as a rule of thumb, mid-December thru February are not the best times to plan a digging expedition. The mines are open and accessible, but the scenery and weather are stunningly beautiful during the rest of the year!

Many locals think that digging after a rain is a great time. The rain has washed off much surface dirt, and it is easier to see the sparkling glitter of the crystal. However, the red clay is everywhere and almost impossible to wash out of your clothes. Be advised that motel owners don't like red clay clogging their drains. They will most likely provide a bucket of water if you request it.

What To Wear

Protection is the best advice for crystal miners. While it need not be heavy, it should cover all exposed areas. Feet are a priority. Boots of some sort not only protect you from tumbling rock, they stabilize your footing over uneven ground or loose rock. Mines can be dangerous if you are thoughtless about your activities.

1. Ryan's Crystal Mine in Pencil Bluff area.

Lighter weight gloves allow you to feel your rock and rub some of the clay off your find. However, light weight gloves are sometimes destroyed in one dig. If you have gloves that are comfortable, bring them. The next area to cover is your head. The sun is brutal in a rock pit, and it is important to keep cool and shade your eyes. Covering your arms and legs may be at your discretion, but generally long pants keep you from rock or crystal bruises, and a light-weight long-sleeved shirt keeps the sun and bugs off you. Of course, in cooler weather dress accordingly!

Mining of Crystals

Crystals are removed from the earth in a number of ways. Depending on your philosophy, it could make a difference in where you dig or where you buy your crystals. Commercial miners frequently use dynamite and blast large well-placed fissures near the veins. This is necessary to move tons of rock that may be covering a particularly rich pocket. They are then able to begin digging with a track-hoe, back-hoe or bull-dozer. Most commercial operations utilize large equipment. This is an aid to the rockhound because it is vastly simpler to climb into a six- to ten- foot- deep area and start digging in exposed veins than sit on top of the ground and wonder what's underneath,where it might be located, and then start a deep dig with a trowel!

However, some individuals believe that the frequency of crystals is disturbed in the blasting process and choose to hand dig their own crystal in order to avoid any possible frequency alteration. Many of these people also believe that the process used in cleaning can disturb the resonance. They feel that oxalic acid or any etching solution will alter the quartz. They prefer to rinse their crystals strictly with water. Some even prefer not to use salt water because of its corrosive effects although many authors recommend clean-ing with salt.

You see that there are many choices to be made before you begin to dig. Are you a purist or would you prefer to have much of the initial work done for you? Do you wish to enjoy your crystal for its beauty, or do you have a purpose in mind that necessitates keeping the crystal exactly as it formed in the ground? There are mines that can meet all these needs, and digging your own with a few well chosen questions will provide hours of relaxing and stimulating enjoyment. By far, the majority of crystal diggers will find the variety of mines and crystals for sale in Arkansas to be quite superior. In fact, from a purist point of view, many believe the Arkansas crystal to be of a finer frequency and greater clarity than the Brazilian.

After you decide on a mine, either call the miner or stop by the retail store. It is necessary to sign a liability waiver, pay your fee and get directions to the mine. Mining costs are usually $2.00 to $25.00 for the day, and you can stay until closing. The cost entitles you to dig and keep all the crystals you find. This is a minimal expense when you compare it to the price of crystals.

Digging Tools

Generally, the best digging tool is a screwdriver of medium to large size. Other helpful tools are crowbars for wedging rocks and a claw tool or a pick. (Check a local hardware store). Shovels are good for breaking ground, and a trowel can be useful. If you find yourself without tools, look in your car's trunk. A tire iron and a screwdriver can be the best tools of all. Many mines will supply digging tools, so always check. Be sure to take a container, a bucket or box, to carry your crystals. They will be full of red clay and dirty. So will you!

Fire In The Hole!

You may find yourself out hiking on Forest Service land or prowling around a seemingly deserted area and suddenly hear the shout "Fire In The Hole." DANGER-IMMEDIATE ACTION-MAKE NOISE-MOVE FROM THE AREA QUICKLY. This is the warning that is used by all miners just prior to exploding dynamite. You have only a minute or minutes to respond. Chances are that you have wandered somewhere you don't belong, and you must let the blaster know that you are there in order to protect yourself. Do not expect conversation from him, simply move out of the area. Blasting can shower rock down on you off the side of a mountain. It can impair your hearing. It can do you bodily harm.

I am a curious person and I live here, so -you guessed it- I have heard the ominous cry. Believe me—once bitten, twice shy. Stay off private property and if you hear shouting, treat it as if blasting is imminent!

Types of Crystal in Arkansas

Courtesy of Arkansas Geological Commission
By J. Michael Howard

The major portion of the quartz in the Ouachita Mountains occurs as white or milky veins. The principal difference between milky quartz and clear rock crystal is the presence of innumerable microscopic bubbles or fluid-filled cavities in the former. These cavities scatter the light that otherwise would pass through as in clear crystal.

Aside from the well -known rock crystal, other varieties of quartz may be found in this region. Smoky quartz is present adjacent to Cretaceous igneous rocks near Magnet Cove in Hot Spring County. The dark color is due to defects in the crystal lattice caused by radioactivity that was present when the quartz was deposited. Banding or growth zoning is not uncommon in well formed crystals from this area. Quartz with water bubbles or fluid inclusions and negative crystal quartz are found near the edges or fringes of the area of major quartz deposition. Generally, these types of quartz resemble quartz from near Herkimer, New York and form in calcite veins which are commonly weathered to clay, leaving the crystals suspended in clay where they wash out in loose soil. Phantom or zoned quartz is caused by temporary interruption of the growth process. Phantoms may be caused by small bubbles or inclusions of minerals adhering to the crystal faces.

Amethyst (purple or bluish-violet quartz) occurs associated with Cretaceous igneous intrusive rocks, particularly as veins with calcite at the Crater of Diamonds State Park and as veins associated with serpentine bodies in northern Saline County. Across the northern limits of vein quartz deposition (see map), a type of quartz termed "solution quartz" by local collectors occurs. This quartz is unusual because much of it has grown as suspended or unattached crystals or clusters (burrs) in a clay-like material called rectorite. When rectorite is fresh, it has much of the appearance of petroleum jelly, but when it drys out rectorite has the consistency of leather. It may weather to a tan or brown color. Specimens of these more unusual varieties are prized by collectors because of their beauty and scarcity.

Several minerals are associated with the quartz, which usually constitutes 90 percent or more of the cavity fillings. Clay minerals, including dickite and nontronite, are widespread. Calcite is a common associate, especially in the parts of the veins cutting limestone or calcareous siltstone. Adularia and chlorite are found in veins cutting certain shales. Carbonaceous material also is common. Less common accessory minerals are brookite, rectorite, the sulfides of lead, zinc, antimony and mercury, the lithium mica cookeite, and the carbonates ankerite and siderite.

Ed. Note: Arkansas produces clear quartz of varying grades. It also grows native "water crystal," a form of anhydrous quartz, and phantoms of varying colors with several types of mineral inclusions. Jewelry points are abundant. Single and double-terminated points range from inch size to many pounds. Tabular crystals or "tabbies" are flat crystals and are fairly common. It is not unusual to find crosses made of any of the above combinations.

Clusters range from perfect, clear miniatures the size of a quarter to slabs the size of a table. These clusters may include phantoms, tabbies, doubles and crosses. If you are familiar with crystal terminology, you will also note an abundance of record-keepers and channeling crystals.

Effects Of Mining

Crystal mines are known to have certain effects on sensitive people. While many will exclaim, " Bah–Humbug!" I include this section for those who will benefit from the information. It comes from my own experience.

I have found that sensitive individuals may experience physical discomfort after a period of time in a mine. Where it hits you will depend on your own system. I, for example, upon first mining, experienced headache although I had no stress or symptoms of illness. I noted this, but did not give it much attention.

At a later time, I took my children, then seven and sixteen, -on a digging expedition. It was cool and about six P.M.–no sun to blame the effects on. After about an hour of exciting digging adventures, we started home. The older immediately began to complain of stomach ache while the younger started to whine about a headache! Now I started to pay attention.

I have since had numerous folks come to my door (they just seem to wind up there).In conversation they mention that their allergies haven't bothered them for years, but they hoped they weren't getting sick. Actually they felt good-except for the headache /stomach ache. Here's what I think happens.

When a person fasts on either juice or water, or diets by eating nothing, the body (generally the liver) begins to release stored toxins. For the first few days of the fast you feel headachy and generally crummy while the system is releasing and flushing toxins. After the initial period, you feel great–"like-a-million-bucks!" That's how the mine or any concentrated amount of crystal works on the emotional or subtle bodies. Being in the frequency of crystal is like being exposed to bright sunshine or rarefied light. As the subtle bodies begin to release toxins, you feel the effects of the cleansing as achiness. After one or more experiences, you will find the discomfort lessens or disappears.

4. *OWNING YOUR OWN MINE*

Amended Land & Resource Management Plan
Ouachita National Forest
Courtesy of U.S. Department of Agriculture

Quartz minerals on the Ouachita National Forest are administered by the USDA, Forest Service under Title 36 of the Code of Federal Regulations part 228 "C", in accordance with Section 323 of Public Law 100-446, enacted on September 27, 1988. Prior to that date, the quartz resource on the Ouachita National Forest in Arkansas had been administered under both the locatable and the leasable minerals programs and involved up to three different federal agencies. Quartz is now administered solely by the local Ouachita National Forest District Ranger. Section 323 of P.L. 100-446 also provides for a consistent and fair revenue generating process which returns 50 percent of the revenues raised from quartz sales back to the State of Arkansas for local county road and school programs.

The principal Ranger Districts involved with quartz sales under this program are the Womble, Jessieville, Winona, Oden and Caddo Ranger Districts. In 1989, these Ranger Districts developed more than 158 quartz contracts for parcels each covering primarily from 10 to 40 acres of Forest lands. The first competitive quartz sale held in June 1989 from bonus bids and from annual contract fees was $26,250. Some of this revenue also came from contracts issued to holders of mining claims who had voluntarily relinquished their mining claims for quartz in preference for a quartz contract issued by the Forest.

The process for gaining access to the quartz mineral estate on the Ouachita National Forest is very simple and begins when a person nominates Forest lands they are interested in exploring and/or developing for quartz. Nominations are submitted to the District Ranger and must be accompanied by a bid deposit which is applied toward the nominator's formal bid for the lands he nominated. The District Ranger works with the nominator to parcel the lands of interest into 10 to 80 acre sites and then conducts an environmental analysis on the parcel. The parcel is then made available for sale through a competitive process that is open to the public. The minimum bid on any parcel is $50, and all bids are considered one-time bonus bids. Parcels that are not sold become available for a limited time from the Ranger District's office through a noncompetitive process. A contract is issued by the District for the sold parcel, and the purchaser then pays an annual contract fee based on the number of acres under contract. Contracts are issued for five years and can be extended by the purchaser for additional five-year periods if so desired. A question and answer pamphlet on the procedure is available from the Forest Supervisors office in Hot Springs.

2. *This is a typical crystal yard.*

5. ROCKHOUNDING IN ARKANSAS

Amended Land & Resource Management Plan
Ouachita National Forest
Courtesy of U.S. Department of Agriculture

Rockhounding and mineral specimen collecting on the Ouachita National Forest is considered to be a recreational activity involving the occasional removal of small amounts of material by hand from surface exposures of rock and quartz veins. Such material obtained in this manner should be for personal use only and cannot be sold. Rockhounding under this condition does not include excavating or any kind of digging to expose quartz crystal bearing veins. The recreational removal of material from lands already under contrac is considered to cause no adverse environmental impact from rockhounding activities on the Ouachita National Forest. However, if persons and groups are interested in pursuing a short-term organized recreational rock- collecting activity on the Forest that may result in access and excavation impacts, they can submit their proposal in writing to the District Ranger for consideration. Any such activity approved by the District Ranger may require the submission of a reclamation bond.

6. CLEANING CRYSTALS

An Interview with Cheryl Ryan

Cheryl, you and your husband, Vernon, have been digging crystals for about three years. The two of you do all your cleaning, as well as all your digging, personally. When you bring crystals home, what is the first thing you do with them in preparation to clean them?

We have wood frame tables with a screen top so that the clay rinses off the rocks and goes through the screen.

That's the kind of thing someone could do very easily on a small scale at home. Use a couple of 2x4's and put some screen over the top of them.

Yes. Wash the clay off the rocks and you usually want to hose them off with the garden hose. I take the smaller pieces and do them by hand, usually with a tub of water and a tooth brush to get the clay off. Then I use dental tools to take the clay out of the crevices that you can't get to with the tooth-brush.

Do you do that right away, or do you let them sit before you start working on them?

It's better to spray them and then let them dry. Then you can get some of the dry clay off with the dental tools and spray them again. We spend a lot more time on the cleaning end than most other people. Usually they use high pressure sprayers and just keep spraying them until they are clean. The nice thing about this method is that if you find one that you really, really like yourself– like I usually do–you can start your own private collection. I have one going now.

You use dental tools to get into the crevices and get pieces of clay out?

Yes, because they are nice and sharp. And they are tiny and pointed.

Do you wear gloves and do you have to take any precautions?

I usually just wear those brown jersey gloves. They get wet and sloppy, but at least you don't cut your fingers and you can hold on to the rocks better and get a better grip on them.

Do you find that just water and picking out clay with dental tools takes care of it, or are there circumstances where you have to go farther than that?

You mean before you put them in the acid? When you get all the clay off, then you put them in oxalic acid which is mixed with water. It's usually best to do that in some kind of big tub or tank. You put a fire underneath it to get it warm and then you let them set. We let ours set for a day, and then the next day we take them out and rinse them off. But if you don't get the clay off, the oxalic acid will not take it off. It's still there and it usually messes the crystals up.

Can you burn your hands on the oxalic acid? Do you have to be careful of that?

You have to wear rubber gloves. It's not good to get on your skin. It gets kind of hot. Also, it's best to clean them outside or in a well ventilated area in order to avoid inhaling the fumes.

Could someone who is doing this at home use a crock pot or something they could heat up without having a big tub with a fire?

Yes, you could use a crock pot.

It strikes me that if you did that, you might have one of these little strainer baskets that you could lift out so that you could use your acid more than once. Do you find that you can use your acid again and again?

Yes. We use ours quite a few times before we change it. It will last quite awhile as long as you keep it covered.

You keep fire under it the entire time the rocks are in the acid?

Usually.We start it one morning and rinse them off the next morning.

Is rinsing an important process?

Yes. You have to be sure to get all of the residue that is left on them from the acid off because it will leave a film on them if you don't.

Do you have to rinse them immediately? You don't want to let them dry with the acid on them?

No. You don't let it dry on there. Then you let them dry in the sun before you box them up. Pick out all the ones you want for yourself.

When you are mixing the oxalic acid with the water, any idea how much you use?

One pound to five gallons of water or one ounce to a quart.

When you are putting your crystals into the acid, do you just dump them all in?

No. You have to put the crystals in baskets, and then we sit the entire basket down inside the acid. You have to be careful not to let them bang against each other because when you get the clay off of them then they are easier to fracture. So you have to be very careful about laying them in the baskets, and then you just set the whole basket down in the vat.

Do you buy oxalic acid right here in town?

I'm sure people can buy small amounts from some of the crystal dealers in town. The first acid we bought was in a coffee can from Ocus Stanley.

Do you have some crystals that you don't put in the acid that come clean enough just by hand ?

Yes. The smoother points don't usually have to because you can get all the clay and stuff off them and they are just perfect.

7. QUARTZ FESTIVAL

Quartz,Craftz & Quiltz is the Mount Ida Fall Festival which is held the third week-end in October each year. A craft and quilt fair is held for three days at the county fair grounds in Mt. Ida accompanied by much festivity, music and food. The focus of the fair is a three- day crystal dig. The cost to dig is approximately $30.00 for the week-end, and the prizes are both cash and crystals. Of course, you can keep everything you dig. Several mines are opened for the dig, and you have your choice of locations. The Mt. Ida Chamber of Commerce is the best contact for information(501-867-2723). If you are new to crystals or wish to see the majority of Arkansas' crystal dealers and rock at one place, this is a treasure of a festival! During the day you can dig or buy from the many crystal booths and exhibits at the fair grounds. At night you can enjoy entertainment on the town square or in the new Roosevelt Performing Arts Auditorium.

3. Stanley's Fold located six miles from Mt. Ida.

8. STANLEY'S FOLD

Stanley's Fold is a fascinating rock formation located only about a mile off Hwy. 270 in Hurricane Grove (about six miles from Mt. Ida). It was named after Ocus Stanley, the grandfather of the crystal business in the area.

Have you ever seen hot Turkish Taffy being made? It folds back and forth over itself in serpentine layers. Now imagine that in rock! Thousands of years ago during a period of geological upheaval, the layers of sandstone folded and curved over each other in a process which indicated both heat and movement.

To get to the fold, look for the Lake Ouachita Inn on the left coming from Hot Springs. Continue on for .5 miles to a road on the left. This road is just past the airport which is also on the left. To reach the fold from Mt. Ida, begin at the Mt. Ida Cafe and go 6.2 miles to the road on the right. Turn and go exactly 1 mile. Look on the right side of the road along the bank. The fold is visible here and becomes more dramatic about 200 feet farther down the road. Other folds exist in the area. A notable one can be seen from the water on the Army Corps' "Geo-Float" trip.

Ouachita Geo–Float Trail
Information Courtesy of the Army Corps of Engineers
Welcome to a region where, 250 to 300 million years ago, the earth's surface was bent, twisted, and deformed in ways that still baffle professional geologists. The self-guided Ouachita Geo-Float Trail takes you, in your own boat, across the waters of Lake Ouachita to some of the most unique geologic features in the world.

As the seasons change, so do the natural features of Lake Ouachita. During the fall and winter months it is easier to view the geologic features because the level is low, but remember, low water levels can make boating hazardous because rocks, stumps, and other obstructions are closer to the surface and the bottom of your boat! Also watch the weather, the time of day, and the gas gauge. Safe boating will make your day more enjoyable.

The Ouachita Geo-Float Trail includes many unique geologic features on the lake but by no means points out all the interesting natural features you will see. The trail is a 16-mile (25.7 km) trip from the Spillway Recreation Area to Brady Mountain Recreation Area and will take about 1 1/2 hours to complete. The time will vary depending on your boat's speed and the time you spend at each stop.

9. CRYSTAL SHOPS

With a few exceptions, all the rock shops listed below are located on Highway 270 between Hot Springs and Mount Ida. One exception is Coleman's, which has three shops in the Hot Springs area; the main shop is located on route 7 north going toward Jesseville. Heartland Crystal and Wegner's Mines are located on the Crystal Loop described in the **Crystal** section. Any name which indicates" call" or" write" will not be located on Hwy. 270.

"Dig your own" mines are listed below, but it is always necessary to check into the shop first or call the miner to sign waivers and get directions to the mine. Fees for digging vary. For example, Wegner's charges $6.00 a day and Coleman's and Robin's $10.00. Each mine is free for children under a certain age. Ocus Stanley & son charges a donation at the discretion of the miner and a deposit on the key. No extra charge is made for crystals found.

A special tip for first -time crystal hunters: if you see a crystal you like anywhere always ask if it's for sale. On my first trip to Arkansas, I found myself in someone's backyard which was full of crystal tables. At the time I thought that it was "private stock." Little did I realize that every bit of the crystal was for sale. All I had to do was ask. It is notable that the dealer did not offer any encouragement or information. Because I did not know how to play the game or ask how to play it, we both lost. Always ask, and always make an offer. You may be pleasantly shocked at the results!

Crystal Sales & Mining
Arrow Head Mining Co.-Mt. Ida,867-2897(call or write)
Coleman Crystal Mines- Jesseville, 984-5328,Retail, Wholesale,Digging, Camping, Showers.
Crystal City-Mt. Ida(3 mi. east),867-3664. Wholesale Only.
Crystal Classics-Mt. Ida, 867-2439,Retail, Wholesale, Appt. Only.
Crystal Hill's Mining- Mt. Ida(5 mi. east), 867-3866,Retail, Wholesale,Digging.

Crystal Mountain Rock Shop-Royal,(20 mi. W. of Hot Springs),Retail, Wholesale.

Crystal Pyramid-Mt. Ida, & Hot Springs,623-2620

Crystal Springs Mining Co.-Crystal Springs,991-3282

Fiddler's Ridge -Mt. Ida(7 mi. east), 867-2314, Retail, Wholesale,Digging.

Forgotten Aye Mines-867-3708. Call, Large points & clusters,Digging.

Heartland Crystal Institute-Mt. Ida(Crystal Loop), 8673412, Retail,Wholesale,Information

Lake Ouachita Inn & Gift Shop-Mt.Ida,867-2643, Retail, Wholesale.

Manley Mining Co.-Mt. Ida. (call 867-2530).

Mountain Gems-Mt. Ida(1 mi. west), 867-2523, Retail, Whole-sale.

Mystic Mountain Crystals-Mt. Ida, 867-3921, Retail, Whole-sale.

Ocus Stanley & Son-Mt. Ida, 867-3556,Retail, Wholesale, Digging, Museum.

Robins Mining Co.-Mt. Ida, 867-2530, 867-2778. Retail, Wholesale,Digging.

Ryan Mines-Pencil Bluff,326-4685,Wholesale,Digging(By Appt.).

Starfire Mines-Mt. Ida(12 mi. east), 867-2431,Retail, Wholesale,Digging.

Wanda's Gift House-Mt. Ida,867-2975.

Wegner Quartz Crystal Mines-Mt. Ida,867-2309, Retail, Wholesale,Digging,Camping.

White Phantom Mine-On the Crystal Loop, Drop in.

Wright's Rock Shop-Hot Springs, 767-4800, Retail, Whole-sale.

10. VORTEX AREAS IN THE OUACHITAS

Throughout history and perhaps throughout your life, occasionally you find yourself in a natural setting which gives you goose bumps or feels warmer or cooler than the surrounding area. Perhaps it is a sensation of grandeur or a distinct impression that you can imagine the people who lived there and toiled to make that place special. Put simply, these spots have a unique energy all their own. The American Indians have called them power spots, areas in which you feel you gain a stronger sense of your connection with the earth or with God.

Physicists can measure magnetic energy and electric energy, each of which can be stronger in some places than others. There are many areas in this country that have such unusual energy that you can stand at almost 45 degrees to the ground and not fall over. Such places are usually tourist attractions called "mystery spots" or some such name. The energy that runs through the Ouachitas is not like the "mystery spots" but more like the power spots the Indians have identified. When you consider the amount of quartz lying beneath the surface and the electrical frequency properties that this mineral contains, it is not unusual that this area lends itself to a number of energy sites or vortexes.

Directions to various areas are provided. Use them as a general guide to find what appeals most to you. I always prefer to find a wonderful place and then form opinions based on my personal experience which I am willing to share with you. Please share yours with me by either writing or stopping by the Heartland Crystal Institute. There are many ways to perceive vortexes, and I find it convenient to think of those in the Ouachitas as being similar to the energy centers located in the body. These centers have been defined scientifically as corresponding with the endocrine glands and have been identified by Eastern philosophy for centuries. They lie along the spine beginning at the tailbone and going to the crown of the head.

4. View from Queen Wilhelmina Scenic Drive (Crown Vortex).

The vortexes run in an east to west direction encompassing almost the entirety of the Ouachita Mountain Range. They begin with the base point in Magnet Cove and move to the "crown" at the summit of Rich Mountain in Queen Wilhelmina State Park. To the east of this range the land flattens out into the lowlands which border the Mississippi, and to the west the terrain quickly drops to the plains which predominate the landscape until you reach the Rocky Mountains. In fact the Ouachitas are the highest point between the Alleghenies and the Rockies. It is the only mountain range in the country that runs east and west versus north and south.

Area 1, the Base, is located in the vicinity of Magnet Cove approximately 20 miles east of Hot Springs. This area is mineral rich and derives its name from the Magnetite found in the area. The magnetic properties of the locale afford a great grounding effect and a distinct blending with the earth.

Area 2, the Generative Center, is the Valley of the Vapors or Hot Springs itself. See the next section on Hot Springs vortexes or the section on **Hiking** for suggestions that might appeal in this area. It is interesting that this area was sin city in the thirties and forties, quite in keeping with the lower aspects of the generative center. The higher aspects, however, point toward creativity and the generation of high potential. This is the focus of Hot Springs growth patterns today.

Area 3,the Solar Plexus Center, is found in the vicinity of Blakely Dam. Ouachita State Park, the Spillway, and Balanced Rock(see **Hiking**) are all in this area. It may prove worthwhile to spend some time on the dam itself reflecting on the issues of personal power and holding back versus letting flow.

Area 4, the Heart Center. Energy begins around the Charlton Recreation area. As you travel west, you pass a Forest Service road on the left that goes to the Crystal Rec. area and Collier Springs. This road travels through the major crystal bearing ranges. (See Crystal Loop.) When you pass over the Montgomery County line, you are within two miles of the turn to the right that leads to Hickory Nut Mountain Rec.area and Lake Ouachita Vista scenic overlook. The overlook is at the top of the mountain and drops off on either side. It is graveled and open and so it may not appear idyllic. BUT the feel is one of complete balance of polarities. It offers not only a balance of opposites, but also of the lower and upper energy centers. Note: Little Missouri Falls has a similar function.

Area 5, the Throat Center, opens before you as
traverse the bridge between Shangri-La and Denby
Lodge on Hwy. 270. You need only start across the opening
to feel the freedom of speech and heartfelt truth that resides
in this area. Denby Point is a resort directly on the point of this
area, and the Denby Point Campground is also within a
quarter mile on the same road. When I first visited the
Ouachitas, I spent my first night in Hot Springs, several nights
at Ouachita State Park, and the rest of my time at Denby Point
(See back cover for **Denby Point Lodge.)**

Area 6, the Brow Center, is atop a mountain, of course.
Which mountain may be up to your discretion. I have found
High Peak, located on the Crystal Loop, to resemble Mayan
centers I have visited. On High Peak there is a sense of
alignment with the earth, the body centers and stellar centers. Other mountains in the area that may serve a similar
function would be Blow-out mountain and Buck Knob. Both
are located north of Pencil Bluff on Hwy. 270 going toward Y
City.See the following section on the **Crystal Loop** for
directions to High Peak.

Area 7, the Crown Center, becomes obvious as you climb
Hwy. 88 outside of Mena to the top of Rich Mountain in Queen
Wilhelmina State Park. The whole top of your head opens up.
Even those who are not sensitive find this scenic drive to be
very special. There is a lodge at the park where you can spend
the night, and camping is available. See **Day Trips** for
directions. As an added bonus, you may wish to travel the fifty
mile- long Talimena Scenic Drive to Talimena Oklahoma. This
winds across the top of the mountain and ends just outside
of the Ouachita National Forest.

I would recommend that you visit those centers that
appeal to you or those that correspond with an area you wish
to work on. From High Peak to Little Missouri Falls is less than
twenty miles, and Queen Wilhelmina only another twenty
miles beyond. From Hot Springs to the Spillway and Balanced
Rock is less than five to ten miles depending on your route.
Charlton and Ouachita Vista are only a half hour drive from

downtown Hot Springs. Please address your written or taped experiences to Heartland Crystal at the address on the back of the title page of this book.

11. VORTEX AREAS OF HOT SPRINGS

An Interview with Ben Howard
Golden Eagle Sanctuary

Vortexes are based around hilltops, valleys, around different types of materia like ore deposits, metal deposits and mineral deposits. All vortexes have specific harmonic structures and components. In terms of the vortexes in the Valley of the Vapors, we have a wonderful phenomenon of the waters being collected here in the National Park and 5000 years later coming up out of the ground as hot water. When the Indians used to come and bathe in the healing waters, the whole valley was one steaming "Valley of the Vapors."

The 47 springs which we now have capped off were all opened and freed as a natural energy control. As you came into the valley, you would walk up through the south or come in through the north. You'd approach the valley, and there would be clouds of steam that would flow down and across and through the valley in every direction and hang in the trees. It's interesting that the Hot Springs National Park itself has crystal beds that are associated with the water that is coming from the substrata. As it comes through the sandstone and it dissolves the silicon, it recrystallizes higher up in a new formation of crystalline beds right underneath the mountain that it all started from. Vortexes are attached to that mountain in a horseshoe-like shape, with the two ends of the horseshoe dipping from the north, and the front end facing down to the south. There is a 8-9 mile trail that loops around the horseshoe. It starts along North Mountain, dips down to the valley and then goes straight up to the West Mountain from the sides of Mountain Valley Water It then snakes along the top of the mountain range looping down to Music

Mountain where it turns about face and comes back. My recommendation is to hike that trail in a clockwise direction. It seems to me that the vortex, the whole energy vortex, is entering into this valley in a clockwise direction. As you go around the circuit, you can experience many aspects of different subforces or components of forces around the hills. As you look ou‚t you'll feel them rushing through you from the different viewpoints that you can see.

There are a couple of rock structures (one is Goat Rock and the other one is Balanced Rock)where there aretremendous energy intake and output. The energy input around Balanced Rock, for instance, is kind of neat. It's very, very peaceful and serene in that vortex. The one on Goat Rock is a little more rugged. It's more toward the north. Actually, it's more east, but it's on the northeast face of North Mountain, where the major water activities are taking place. You've got a yin and a yang component across the valley, and incidentally, both of those sites, and particularly the Balanced Rock site date back some 10,000 years when the Indians used to come out here and make the tools of their trade– arrowheads, picks and whatever.

I believe the hot springs to be unique, whether it be in terms of the healing aspects of the water or its ability to flush through toxins. But in terms of just going and grounding out–go up in those hills! There are very special energies there. The West Mountain is a very sacred mountain. Only the Chiefs of the tribe were ever allowed to go up on that mountain. The Sugarloaf Mountain range is very gentle, beautifully gentle, serene and peaceful. Not many people go up there at all. In fact, I've only seen one or two people ever up there on that side of the range. To get back into nature is what we're all about. It's what times are about in terms of healing ourselves and healing Mother Earth at the same time. (See the section on **Hiking**.)

For years I've been hearing about the power of the vortexes in Sedona, and last year I had the opportunity to take a lightning tour. I was amazed at all the information I received sitting on Bell Rock. In comparison, though, you come to Hot Springs and when you sit on a crystal body of rock, it's a very different type of energy field you're on. To me the energies in Sedona were very directly related to the lower astral or spirit worlds. In terms of the crystalline beds, I think, to sum it all up, they are a much higher vibration than other vortexes around the planet. The energies of the crystal beds around here and healing waters are quite special.

12. EARTH CHANGES IN THE OUACHITAS

Excerpted From <u>Visions of a Seer Earth Changes</u>
By Terry

Many Visions

During the course of many life readings, someone will ask,"Where will I be at such and such time"? And as I am lifted up to scan the area of the United States to pinpoint an area of interest to the entity, I sometimes look down and see the Earth's terrain below me as it is at that location and time. It is in an instant that I see the changes that have taken place at that time.

Because of the times that are approaching, I was asked to try and see all of the Earth changes and get some sort of time perspective for the beginning. It was early September 1989, that as six of us were sitting around, that I began my journey. But first, let us go back to when my visions began. St. Augustine, Florida 1987. Sitting in my home and office, feeling relaxed and one with the lady across from me, for whom I was giving a life reading, she asked where she would be during the Earthshift. I was lifted up and while I was scanning the United States, I saw her and her family in the area of North Carolina. Being above the earth, I looked down and saw the entire state of Florida gone, as well as half of south Georgia, Alabama, Mississippi and Louisiana. In their place was a vast expanse of water, and I sensed what had taken place was part of the earth change. I was asked when it was and I was told 1996. No other information was forthcoming at that time, and I didn't pursue the matter; I went ahead with this lady's life reading.

It did not occur to me to question the validity of this information as in the past. I had been charting hurricanes with a pendulum and with an 85 percent accuracy of pinpointing the exact location of landfall and wind speed. I felt what I saw was correct and felt no need for verification. The readings became more and more accurate, and one day, several years ago, I discovered I could read the Akashic records. It was then I started getting information of the future Earth changes.

In August 1988, a friend concerned with relocating his family to a safe place asked me about three states: Arizona, Colorado and Missouri. I saw Arizona as being relatively safe, land wise, but dangerous people wise. I saw thousands of refugees roaming there and destitute of belongings and food. I saw chaos and turmoil. Colorado was again safe land wise, but still I saw severe overcrowding, and I knew it was not right for them. Then looking to the state of Missouri, the third state he had asked about, I saw such a difference in terrain I had to ask for clarification. I was told that because of the flooding of the Mississippi River valley, much of Missouri was dangerous swamp land. It was known, after the shift, to be an area to be avoided.

Floating over the land, I could see much safe land inhabited by groups living in harmony, but surrounded and cut off from other parcels of land by great swamps. Those of you who desire to settle there MUST be there before the shift and settled and at one with your neighbors. Travel will be difficult and possibly impractical for some groups in many localities except for long detours. This will be an area that will have to relearn the methods of supply and demand as our forefathers knew in the pioneer days.

Life In Arkansas

Three months later, in November of 1988, I received a letter from one of my good friends who had moved from St. Augustine to a small area in Northwest Arkansas. She was inquiring about the safety of that area as well as some insights into the past history of the region as she had such a feeling of having lived there before in a past life.

I drifted into the alpha state for a short time and saw the land as it will be after the shift. Areas of the southern half of the state were under water, all the way to Texas. I scanned the eastern half, and it, too, was under the flooding waters. I knew this part was the Mississippi River valley.

I was lifted higher and saw the entire state as a whole and saw what I call North and South Arkansas, as it was divided by a large body of water. After moving to Arkansas, I soon discovered the Arkansas River runs across the state as I had seen it. But I was told it was a safe state for what remained, but stay out of the lowlands around the rivers.

I was immediately taken back into the distant past and saw this land was the northern part of Atlantis– a healing place. A section devoted to the great healing arts of Atlantis. I discovered that I had also been there, as well as other people I had come in contact with throughout the years. I was told that because of this good work the land itself had built up a reserve of good energies and Karma. There were also great breakthroughs with Crystal Healing made here in the way of automated healing devices in crystal chambers.

The New Atlantis

...Being centrally located is also another contributing factor. The positive vibrations of thousands of crystals underground multiplying the vibrations for the safety of all here will certainly play a large part in drawing people here. For centuries, the Indian tribes have held this land sacred and neutral territory.

I don't mean that everyone should be here as there are many safe places, but as to this area being a center or clearing house for communications. This, coupled with the climate change after the shift, would have ideal growing seasons and many cottage type industries and their products. Everything points toward the state of Arkansas as being the center of the new era with regards to the new millennium.

It is important for all of you reading this to understand clearly. The time is near. Don't put it off to the last minute to make your move whatever you decide. Plan your move no later than the end of 1992. Find your space. Settle in. Make provisions for the thousands of others who will be following. Meet your neighbors and establish lines of supply and communications.

13. UNIFIED ENERGY FIELDS

An Interview with Ben Howard
Golden Eagle Sanctuary

Ben, what are Unified Energy Fields?

I've always been attracted to working with crystals. When I was about 18 or 19, I'd have crystals in my pocket, and I used to wave them around my head when I got headaches. As an adult, I decided I'd like to come down here and study with Dr. Randall Bair, who'd been using crystals synergistically energy-wise with several other components. The units that he was building were called unified energy fields, which combine the use of crystals and different shapes. He believed the combinations would augment the effects. What we've been doing is combining the basic building blocks in terms of shape to make them into form energies. We combine a variety of crystals and minerals, color and sound, thereby creating <u>Unified</u> Energy Fields.

Give me an example of the shapes you use to work with people.

The shapes start off with the most simple, which are the circle and the triangle. If we take the circle and triangle and make them into three-dimensional components, we get spheres and tetrahedrons. And then if we take those simple building blocks through different harmonic resonances, they become more complicated in terms of how energy is put together.

Let's make this easy for a reader to understand. Your basic unit that you've just described might be akin to the great pyramid, in terms of having four faces. It sounds to me like you can multiply that. Do you have a simple pyramidal shape, or in fact are these more sophisticated and complicated?

No, I don't think there is anything sophisticated and complicated in terms of shapes. We move from the tetrahedron to the cube, which is a hexahedron, from a four into a six, into the octahedron which is very akin to a pyramid into the icosa and then finally into the dodecahedron. In terms of energy we use the shapes like pieces of sculpture to augment or align, very specifically, the energy fields around us according to those basic component building blocks.

Describe the components. What are the structures made of?

We can make them out of any material. However, the materials that we choose to use are the noble metals: copper, silver and gold, simply because of their resonant harmonics. We could have used wood in terms of the structure and it would have a very resonant, smooth flowing field. We've gone the other way and gone with the metals and said, "Okay, let's use the metals as teaching tools, or experiential tools. We use them as healing tools in terms of exploring and aligning the fields around us and looking at different aspects of the way the universe is built.

What do you utilize besides the noble metals? Do you use crystals, lights, sound, music?

Well, there we get into the whole coloration of these fields. We tune them with specific light and specific color. As for frequency, we use crystals, rocks, different pieces of shell or salt–any of God's components of this universe. We put them into a chamber so the field is resonated to that structure and to that individual inside. One of the major chambers that we have is the receivership chamber and it has a medicine wheel of 24 crystals that are placed directly on a grid around the square of the pyramid structure. These crystals are all laid out on the ground and aligned perfectly to one another. They are balanced in terms of how one across the circle faces the other and in terms of the direction from the north, south, east, west. They are all aligned to bring in the energies that are around this planet and to harmonize with them. The receivership chamber also has 63 gold- plated pyramids that are placed around it. It is basically the intent of the user or operator as to what it will manifest.

Someone's intention as he enters one of these fields may be for healing, for himself or for the planet, may be for balance, for wisdom, or spiritual growth. The structures that you provide not only help focus an individual in that process but focus the frequency or the energy. Is that correct?

It's quite remarkable how well they work and how effective a tool they are. The major attraction that I had toward these particular units was that I felt that I reconnected very, very quickly with aspects of how I felt in the other dimension. An overall concept of intention for me in terms of using the chambers is to help align a person through to their inner voice, their guide, their way for understanding what it is right for them to do at a particular time.

These appear to be very exciting tools! Am I to understand that you have these right here in Hot Springs?

Yes, we have them here and we take them out to fairs. We were on TV earlier this month. It's very exciting to be here in Hot Springs because crystals are the major activation tool around the planet. Many of us feel we are being drawn to this area to help bring that knowledge back. The basic message that I can find which is the basic message that comes out of all of the chambers is that Christ loves them and they should love one another.

When people come into the Hot Springs area, is it possible for them to utilize these chambers?

That's a good question. Over the last year guests have been coming to the Bed & Breakfast that are more in tune than I am. They have said that over the last year there have been dynamic shifts of energy around Hot Springs and around the crystals here. We have a guest at present that says she is amazed that the auras that people carry down here are much larger than they would be back where she is from in New York City. But at the same time, the crystals and the interface of the energy fields around us amplify whatever attitude that we're locked into. It will make it tougher for some and more enlightening for others, depending on where you want to be.

Is your Bed & Breakfast, which is also a wholistic center, open to the public?

Totally open to the public. The people that have been coming to us are from all walks of life. We have a workshop the third weekend of every month. We have visiting lecturers, speakers,seers and North American Indians.   I'm giving classes which I call Sacred Sciences. The current session is the "Hot Springs Connection Workshop Series." I am a mining engineer and so I just fell in love with linking together the science and the sacredness of the structure and finding that truly there is an embodiment of both in one. It would be preferable for someone who wants to come see the chambers to give me a call and set up an appointment.

14. THE CRYSTAL LOOP

The Crystal Loop is a circular drive of about thirteen miles that passes by Robins' Mine, Wegner's Mine & Campground, Heartland Crystal Institute, several mines up on the mountain, the Crystal Mountain Scenic Area, Collier Springs, High Peak and the Crystal Recreation area. The Crystal Mountain to High Peak area is particularly good for meditation and communion with nature. It traverses an area noted for crystal and is one of the most gorgeous drives in Montgomery County. The road is mostly gravel, a Forest Service road, but is kept in good enough shape that a passenger car can travel it without harm. Perhaps caution should be exercised after heavy rains or winter storms.

5. Crystal caves such as this are found in the Crystal Loop area.

To enjoy this area, turn south on Hwy. 27 in Mt. Ida where it T's off of Hwy. 270. Travel 4 miles and turn left at the Wegner Crystal Mines sign. It is best to set your odometer on 0 to best use the following directions.

.00   Turn left on Owley Rd. At Wegner sign.
.9   Robins' Mine. Do not enter unless authorized.
2.0   Wegner's Wholesale.
2.1   Heartland Crystal Institute.
2.5   Keep left.
3.1   Wegner's Retail & Campground.
4.0   Keep right.
4.4   Keep left–don't cross bridge.
5.7   White Phantom Mine.
5.8   Stop sign. Forest Service road 177 runs left to Alamo, the airport and the Garland County line. Turn right to Collier Creek and the Crystal Loop. This area is the Crystal Mountain Scenic area.
6.2   Keep right.

7.3   Straight.
9.1   Turn left on 177K to High Peak about a mile) or straight
        to Crystal Recreation Area.
10.8   Crystal Recreation Area. Good hiking here.
13.6   Rejoin Hwy. 27. Turn left to Norman 2 miles or right to
        Mt. Ida 6 miles.

15. LITTLE MISSOURI FALLS

One of the loveliest day trips is to the Little Missouri Falls in the Albert Pike Recreation Area. It is managed by the U.S. Forest Service and camping is available. Little Missouri Falls is a day recreation area that closes for the night, but it is well worth a visit. I lived here for eight months before I discovered it, but it is a treasure that many visitors and residents alike will appreciate. The cover picture on this book is of the falls at the "Little Mo". It is a series of cascading water falls tumbling through high rock walls. Swimming is possible and hiking available in either short or long treks. It is easily reachable in a passenger car although caution should be exercised after extremely heavy rains.

For those who search out energy spots on the earth, this one is a dandy. In fact, please write me of your experiences here. It seems to be a place of great balance, one in which opposite polarities are brought into harmony. However, it also takes you right out of yourself—much like a roller-coaster into the heart and whooshes you out the crown. The experience will vary with the individual, but this area can align the upper centers with the subtle bodies. Many will feel the presence of a peaceful heart in this vortex.

To get to the "Little Mo" turn south on Hwy. 27 in Mt. Ida where it T's off of Hwy 270. Travel 9 miles to the stop sign in Norman. Here you continue straight, picking up Hwy. 8. Go 13 miles to the Little Mo entrance sign and turn left. You are now on Forest Service roads. They are well

6. Little Missouri Falls.

marked and generally well kept.Continue straight on this road for 5 miles, and turn right over the small bridge(F.S. 25). It is .8 miles to the left turn into the day use area which is another .2 miles. This last turn can be missed if you are traveling too fast and miss the sign which is angled to face those leaving the falls. A word about dirt roads; they are easy to travel but the five miles seems like twenty five. Be sure to check your odometer to keep accurate track.

For further adventures go back to the road you came in on (turn right on F.S.25 and continue to F.S.43) and turn right. At the T turn right again and you will run into the Albert Pike campgrounds and a small store. For the very adventuresome this is the place to start asking for directions to the Winding Staircase. It is only accessible by four-wheel vehicle and then only in good weather. I have been there within the past two months(Spring '90), but rumor has it that four-wheel drive entrance will be outlawed and foot access will be all that is left. This will make it impossible for most visitors to thread the maze into this idyllic swimming spot, but for those few who are "called," may the force and Indiana Jones be with you!

16. MINERALS IN THE OUACHITAS

Courtesy of the U.S. Forest Service
The following is a list of some of the minerals found in the Ouachita Mountains and approximate locations.

Barite- Pigeon Roost/Glenwood
Bauxite-Bauxite, AR
Coal- Heavner, OK
Gypsum Satin Spar-Murfreesboro
Hematite-Ouachita N.F. High Peak
Magnetite-Magnet Cove
Novaculite-Hot Springs Mountain
Pyrite-Magnet Cove
Tripoli(weathered Novaculite)-west of Myers
Turquoise-Mona Lisa Mine Ouachita N.F.
Variscite-Ouachita N.F.,Malden
Wavelite-Ouachita National Forest(near Avant)

WATERS

17. HOT SPRINGS

Excerpted From <u>Out of the Vapors</u>
By: John C. Paige & Laura Soulliere Harrison
Courtesy of Hot Springs National Park

Geology

The hot springs of Hot Springs National Park are the result of complex natural geological processes. The park is in the Ouachita Mountains of central Arkansas. The topography of the park is mountain ridges running from east to west, intermontane basins, and the piedmont plateau. Hot Springs lies at the southern edge of these ridges. These mountains are mainly of sedimentary composition, encompassing geological formations from the Ordovician (440 million years ago) period and, possibly, as early as the Cambrian (470 million years ago) period. During most of the Paleozoic era (470 to 230 million years ago), what became the Ouachita Mountains lay submerged under an ancient shallow sea that extended from Louisiana to New Hampshire. Approximately 500 million years ago, geological stresses deep in the earth resulted in the exceedingly slow movement of the South American plate northward to collide with the North American plate. This collision of tectonic plates slowly over geological time created the Ouachita Mountains. The enormous pressures of this geological activity caused the shale and sandstone layers to fracture and fissure. These huge rock layers moved up and down along the fault line, causing local relief to vary as much as 1,000 feet.

Over the centuries, rainfall in the area northwest to northeast of the park has percolated down through rock fractures and fissures in the Big Fork formation and Arkansas novaculite where the heat from the interior of the earth warms the water causing it to rise to the surface by way of joints and faults in the Hot Springs sandstone formation. The surface water temperature is more than 140 degrees. This journey from rainwater to spring water takes about 4,000 years. At the surface the water escapes from the ground in both liquid and gaseous forms. The dissolved minerals in the water precipitate to form the white to tan travertine or "tufa rock" seen near the openings of the hot springs. Slightly less than a million gallons of water a day flow from the 47 springs in the park.

The geography has obviously affected the development pattern of the area. All of the springs issue from the west slope of Hot Springs Mountain at a mostly lower level, and originally they drained directly into Hot Springs Creek. In the area making up what is now Bathhouse Row, the creek runs north-south along the base of Hot Springs Mountain through a relatively narrow gorge that is between Hot Springs Mountain and West Mountain. The remaining floodplain is relatively flat and has been used as a major thoroughfare since the early 19th century. The road originally crossed and recrossed Hot Springs Creek several times, but the channeling of Hot Springs Creek in the latter part of the century resulted in straightening the road. The limits on the immediate vicinity posed by the geography only allowed for a linear north-south development.

History of Spas

At the beginning of the 20th century, promoters of the spa at Hot Springs, Arkansas, claimed that the bathhouses there served people from around the world and that the curative abilities of that southern spa's waters were of worldwide renown. These claims, however, require careful analysis to evaluate their validity and to properly understand the place of Hot Springs in the broader context of European and United States spa history.

The practice of traveling to hot or cold springs in hopes of effecting a cure of some ailment dates to prehistoric times. Archaeological investigations near hot springs in France and Czechoslovakia revealed Bronze Age weapons and offerings. In Great Britain, ancient legend credited early Celtic kings with the discovery of the hot springs at Bath, England.

Some of the earliest written descriptions of western bathing practices came from Greece. The Greeks began bathing regimens that formed the foundation for modern spa procedures.The Romans emulated many of the Greek bathing practices. These Roman baths varied from simple to exceedingly elaborate structures, and they varied in size, arrangement, and decoration. In taking a Roman bath, the bather induced sweating by gradually exposing himself to increasing temperatures. To accommodate this ritual, all Roman bathhouses contained a series of rooms which got progressively hotter. Most contained an apodyterium—a room just inside the entrance where the bather stored his clothes. Next, the bather progressed into the frigidarium (cold room) with its tank of cold wate, t"he tepidarium (warm room), and finally the caldarium (hot room). The caldarium, heated by a brazier underneath the hollow floor, contained cold-water basins which the bather could use for cooling. After taking this series of sweat and/or immersion baths, the bather returned to the cooler tepidarium for a massage with oils and final scraping with metal implements. Some baths also contained a laconicum (a dry, resting room) where the bather completed the process by resting and sweating.

By the beginning of the 19th century the Europeans' bathing regimen consisted of numerous accumulated traditions. The bathing routine included soaking in hot water, drinking the water, steaming in a vapor room, and relaxing in a cooling room In addition, doctors ordered that patients be douched with hot or cold water and given a select diet to promote a cure. Authors began writing guidebooks to the health resorts of Europe explaining the medical benefits and social amenities of each. Rich Europeans and Americans traveled to these resorts to take in cultural activities and the baths.

7. The Fordyce Bathhouse on Bathhouse Row.

18. BATHHOUSES

A hot bath is more a procedure than a place–one that makes you feel like "a million bucks." Generally the bathhouse is located on one of the floors of a hotel. Once inside you are given a private place for undressing and storing your clothes. Next, you are wrapped in a sheet–Greek tunic style. A private soak, whirlpool, if you wish, sitz-bath, steam cabinet, hot towel wrap, cool down and optional massage are the ingredients of the experience! Prices are very reasonable–in the $10.00 range, and the process takes about an hour.

The traditional bath is males separated from females and is the predominant style in all hotels and bathhouses. However, co-ed family-style bathing is available at the Hot Springs Health Club on the ground floor of the Libby Memorial Hospital. This facility is open seven days a week from 9A.M. to 9P.M., and the entrance fee of $9.00 allows you to spend as long as you wish providing you don't leave and then return. Ask about their membership rates. They feature two weight -training and exercise rooms, several tubs of varying temperatures, bubble pools, two saunas and full sized heated pools on the lower floors. They have dressing rooms and lockers and will provide bathing suits, if necessary.

The traditional bath personally pampers you and assures you're bathing in water and tubs that have been cleaned and filled just for you. However, it's over in one hour and you can't share the experience. Family-style bathing lets multi-generational groups enjoy bathing together with conversation and laughter for as long as you wish, but you will be bathing with many other people and sharing the water. I personally enjoy both types.

Bathhouse Listings

United States Department of the Interior/National Park Service
Hot Springs National Park, Arkansas

The bathhouses listed below are furnished with thermal water from Hot Springs National Park in accordance with contracts or permits of the Department of the Interior, National Park Service. Approved bath rates include tub and sitz bath, vapor cabinet and hot packs.

Buckstaff 623-2308	Bathhouse Row	Weekdays:	7-11:45 a.m. 1:30 - 3 p.m.
		Saturdays:	7-11:45 a.m.
Arlington Hotel 623-7771	Central & Fountain	Weekdays:	7- 11:30a.m. 1:30 - 4 p.m.
		Saturdays:	7-11:30 a.m. 1:30-3:30 p.m.

Downtowner 135 Central   Weekday: 7-11:30 a.m.
Motor Inn   1:30-3:30 p.m.
624-5521   Saturday: 7-11:30 a.m.

Park Hilton   305 Malvern   Weekday: 7-11:30 a.m.
623-6600   Saturday: 4 - 9 p.m.
                               Sunday: 7-11 a.m.

Majestic   Park &   Weekday 6:30-11:30 a.m.
Hotel   Central   4:30-9 p.m.
623-5511   Saturday:6:30-11:30 a.m.
                               Sunday: 6:30-11:30 a.m.

The following facility has Thermal water whirlpools, Hot tubs,
Universal gym & Saunas, Co-ed bathing.

Hot Springs   500 Reserve   Weekday: 9 a.m.- 9 p.m.
Health Spa   Weekend: 9 a.m.- 9 p.m.
321-9664

19. THERMAL WATER DISTRIBUTION

Water from 44 of the hot springs is piped by gravity flow
into the 300,000- gallon reservoir beneath Park Headquarters. The pumps in the Headquarters' basement pump part of
this water through a 10-inch pipeline along the front of
Bathhouse Row. The water flowing into the reservoir which is
not pumped out again is passed on as overflow into Hot
Springs Creek. The bathhouses take off part of the hot water
from the 10-inch main, part is diverted to the various thermal
fountains, and part is pumped to the 400,000 gallon reservoir and the 1000,000- gallon high-level reservoir on Hot
Springs Mountain. The remainder of the water goes on to the
Heat Exchanger. Here it is cooled somewhat by passing
through radiators. During the summer months, when the air
temperature is high, the air-cooling system is supplemented
by a water- cooling system. The hot water passes through

large cylinders containing pipes filled with cold well water. The heat then passes from the hot water to the cold water without any mixing of the two systems. The cooled water is then pumped back along Bathhouse Row, where the bathhouses take off part of it and the remainder is pumped to a 100,000- gallon holding reservoir on Hot Springs Mountain.

The holding reservoirs are used to provide water to the outlying bathhouses when the pumps are shut off. This water is pumped to the reservoirs and flows out again, through the same pipes.

An average of 10,000,000 gallons of water is pumped each month. Flow meters located at each bathhouse send electrical impulses to receivers located in the Headquarters' basement. These receivers then record on graphs the amount of water being used.

20. COLD SPRINGS

Although the hot springs receive the majority of the attention, the cold springs in the area are also utilized by many for drinking and health purposes. In downtown Hot Springs there is a cold water spring (66 degrees) on Whittington Avenue. Three Sisters Spring is located in the Ouachita State Park just beyond Blakely Dam. The Three Sisters are three springs that all flow into this area of the park. If you are curious or interested, take a clean bottle and sample the waters. In Montgomery County just south of Mount Ida is Collier Springs. This cold spring is located in a beautiful woodland setting on the "Crystal Loop".(See **Crystal** Section.) It is situated in a picnic area and flows through crystal country just below the the High Peak.

<u>Montgomery County</u> *Our History*

can be purchased at
Wacaster Oil Co. in Mt. Ida

8. Collier Cold Springs Located on the Crystal Loop.

21. HISTORY OF LAKE OUACHITA

**Excerpted From Montgomery County Our History
By Debbie Scott Baldwin**

The creation of the largest lake in Arkansas has made quite a difference in our county's prosperity and progress. Some believe Mount Ida would have been a ghost town in 1986 if Lake Ouachita had not been formed. Some county residents are still bitter today because the government condemned their land or their parents' land and forced them to relocate. Most people thought it would never happen. Many years passed, and the lake and dam were still just facts on paper. Montgomery County property owners lived as if their homes and farms would never be taken from them by the flooding waters of a lake.

Over 115 years ago Congress authorized the first survey made on the Ouachita River. This survey was made to determine what, if anything, the government should do to reduce flood hazards and aid navigation. It was found that the steep incline caused much variation in the streamflow. The steep descent from Blakely Mountain to Arkadelphia, a distance of seventy-five miles, caused the river to drop 228 feet. But, from Arkadelphia to Camden, a distance of sixty-five miles in level terrain, the river only dropped 82.5 feet. Streamflow varies from as little as eighty-five cubic feet per second to as much as 107,000 cubic feet per second.

Problems concerning the river confronted many sessions of Congress. Also, many surveys were made of the river by private as well as public agencies, and millions of dollars were spent before even a suitable dam site was chosen. It was not until 1910 that any thought was given to developing the power resources of the river, but even then such an undertaking was not considered valuable enough to be financed by the government alone. Later studies revealed that development of this power should be underwritten by a private company. As a result, Arkansas Power and Light Company became interested. However, nothing was done for several years until Harvey Couch and Arkansas Power and Light began to carry out plans to harness the great Ouachita. Engineers walked many miles on the river's banks searching for possible dam sites. In 1920 Arkansas Power and Light began buying river bottom land for its planned reservoir.

In 1923, work on the first of three dams was begun. Remmel Dam, completed at a cost of $1,600,000, created Lake Catherine, named for Harvey Couch's daughter. It has an area of 3,000 acres. The second dam, Carpenter, cost $7,000,000 and created a 7,150 acre lake. Lake Hamilton was named for C. Hamilton Moses, a close friend and advisor to Couch. The third and largest dam was to be constructed at Blakely Mountain in Garland County. This dam was to serve three purposes: flood control, the generation of hydroelectric power, and to hold back water for recreational use. The estimated cost to Arkansas Power and Light was over $6,000,000, with the government paying $2,000,000 for the flood control portion of the operation. To this date the federal government had never cooperated with a private utility for the joint purpose of developing water power and creating flood control.

When time came to name the newly formed lake, Couch Lake was suggested to be a memorial to Harvey Couch, for what he had done for home people of Arkansas. The name "Ouachita" was in honor of an ancient Indian tribe that lived along the river. The dedication of the dam was July 4, 1956, and was an elaborate all-day program featuring many celebrities.

The Corps of Engineers has nineteen campgrounds around Lake Ouachita, nine of which are located in Montgomery County. One's choice of accommodations can range from rustic to luxurious condominiums with private Jacuzzi spa, fully equipped kitchens, color cable television and daily housekeeping service.

Fishing is fantastic on Lake Ouachita. The largemouth bass is the most popular species with fishermen. Lunker largemouth are not uncommon, and it also has its share of other bass species. Stripers in the forty pound and over category have been taken here. Other species include smallmouth, bluegill, walleye, crappie and catfish. Also, the Game and Fish Commission has stocked rainbow trout in the lake. Many prestigious fishing tournaments are held on Lake Ouachita each year.

Available at many docks and resorts, one will find boat and motor rentals, guide service, tackle and other gear. The certified scuba diver can find scuba air and a complete dive shop. The lake has something for just about everyone, including tennis, skiing, sailing, and exploring old logging trails and caves. On the shores of Lake Ouachita hikers/tourists find hardwoods, such as red oak, post oak, and hickory within a predominantly pine stand. Mountains surrounding the lake range up to 1,350 feet. The bald eagle and osprey winter around the lake from November through March.

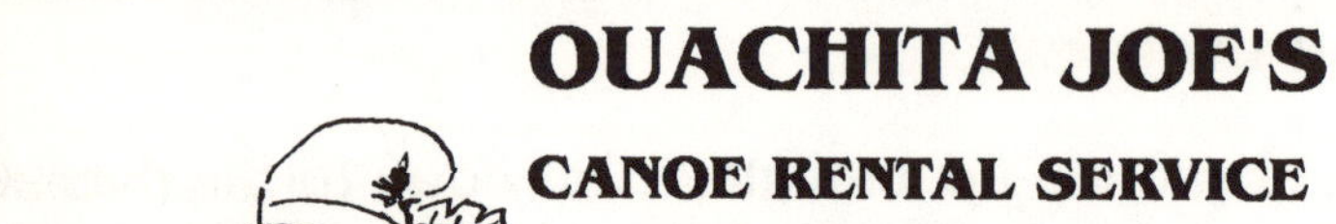

22. CANOEING THE OUACHITA

An Interview with Ouachita Joe
Owner of Ouachita Joe's Canoe Rentals

Talk to me a little bit about the river. Is it the sort of thing that someone who omes from the city can easily adapt to?

This is one of the easiest styles of river there is besides a lake. It's Class I and II. Even now when we've had high rains, it may be a low III. Very simple for even the scaredest of novices to be under control. We've got the shoals; that gives an element of excitement when it drops off in elevation, and it's got still waters. Of course, you've got the trees, birds and flowers, the hills, the eagles in the spring. Last year we had six nesting pair. We've got herons, woodducks, all your king-fishers and turkey.

When people come to float, what kinds of trips do they want to make?

We show them the map, ask them what length of float they want, what type of floaters they are, and what they are interested in. From that we decide on what type of float and the length of it– a 2- hour float all the way up to the 7-hour float. Or they can go on overnight floats and camp on the banks of the shoals. The most popular part is Oden to Rocky Shoals. It's the most scenic and its the most easily accessible. One of the things you might want to include on the Oden to Rocky Shoals float is an old Indian cave, a recess in the rocks. They call it rock house cave. It's just a recession under a rocky ledge.

We load them up and take them down to the river. On the way I explain some of the history of the community, like how Pencil Bluff got its name. The bluffs behind us are all slate. Schools used to, before paper was a commodity, come down, chip off a little slate block, and that was their writing material for classes. Before that it was called Sock City. The locals don't like the story or even the name on the sign at the old grocery store. But in the early days, there was an old bootlegger, and he kept all his money in a sock so that when the sheriff raided him he'd grab his sock and get out the back door. That's how the area got its name. Then when people started settling there, they changed it to Pencil Bluff. Of course, I tell them about Blow-out Mountain. I basically don't know the truth behind it, but it's possible it blew its top and threw rocks all over the county.

What about rapids or shoals?
There's basically no actual rapids, like white waters. We've got shoals that drop in elevation that get real fast. We've got rocks and tree limbs in the river that make it turbulent and that give you excitement. There are some large deep pools of flat water. If you use your common sense, this is one of the safest rivers.

What about kayacking?
It's too rocky with too much underbrush in it, and it doesn't get that deep. The Cossatot is the only place you can kayack. They have restrictions since it became a state park. Canoes are a little bit dangerous for that kind of white water. You know what Cossatot means? It's French for skull crusher. It's a wild river. The upper part of the Cossatat is just like the Ouachita. It's real mild, but you get down to the falls and by then it's class 4 or 5 rapids.

9.Ouachita River photographed from Pencil Bluff.

Tell me a little bit about fishing, and then we'll go on to hiking.

Fishing is excellent here. We have smallmouth, large-mouth, crappie, your small perch. In the early spring you get white bass and walleye, which are running right now, that come out of the lake. It's excellent fishing; we just this last year had two catfish pulled out of the lake just right here below the river and one was 29 and one was 38 pounds. I could put my foot in the 38- pounder's mouth. We have a lot of guides that are fly fisherman that come out and bring their customers to teach them fly fishing. They rent our canoes and go out and they stop along the banks and work their students that way.

Tell me a little bit more about this because I have heard that fly fishing really was ....

Very popular in the rivers. They like the idea of the fast water on the shoals because that's where the smallmouth bass are feeding. We had a man from Fort Smith who was one of our first customers, and he constantly brought his students out here. He wrote us up in his fly fisherman's newsletter. It's getting more and more popular.

What kind of bait would you recommend for someone fishing on this river? Say in the spring.

Your spinners, your Rooster Tails,Rebel, crawfish, minnows. Light bait is always good, minnows and crawfish. Anything will strike at it. Mostly what people come out here for is the bass.Crappie is just something that they get extra. Crappie is great to eat. Most of the people come out here for the smallmouth, because they can get up to 4-5 pound brownies.

What about hiking in the Ouachitas?

You've got the Ouachita trails which are north of us, and you've got the Womble Trails which are on the other side of the river. People hike from the other side of Oden all the way to the 27 Fishing Village. Then it goes north to the Ouachita Trails. It would take about two and one half days to hike from 27 to Rocky Shoals, about two days from Womble at the Tower to Rocky Shoals.You could do the one from the Sims Highway to Rocky Shoals in only a couple of hours. We've had joint hiking and canoeing. We work out individual plans. They can come and hike two days, and then we meet them with the canoe and then they canoe all day, whatever they want to do. It's a pretty popular idea. Hiking and canoeing, the combined idea is getting pretty popular. Had a lot of it last year.

Do people stay here with you or do they....

We have three camp sites that they camp at here. Or they can go to the Forestry campgrounds. Plus there's also camping along the shoals if you really want to get away from it all.

What about seasons on the river?

This is a year-round river. Late summer and early fall, most of your rivers up here are pretty well dried up. We're always floating, year-round. The dogwoods and the apple blossoms bloom in the spring. Summer of course, it's just green and gorgeous. The water is clean and clear. Swimming is real popular here because the water is so clear. In the fall, of course, the colors of the trees change, and that's when our eagles come in.

23. CANOEING—PROFILE OF THE RIVER

An Interview with John Williamson
Owner of Ouachita Heights & Rocky Shoals Canoe

Do you take people up to the headwaters?

The beginning of the Ouachita River is up above Mena, and there is actually a stone up there that marks the headwaters at the very beginning. Actually, the floatable water from where it empties into Lake Ouachita to the headwaters where we start floating is about 67 miles of river. We take them up to the furthermost point that they'd be able to float, which would be above McGuire, which on the highway would be up above Ink. We have places in McGuire, Cherry Hill, Pine Ridge and then Oden. These are our normal stopover places and put- in and take- out spots. Those would be about a one -day float each, 12-14 miles on each stretch.

Now are these private put in places, or are these places where forest service people or campers can put in also if they wished?

Some of it is on forest service land, a couple of places are on private land, but it has been opened to the public for so long that it is considered public access. The Corps of Engineers keeps a little development area, a picnic table, and a road going in that is passable so that people can get in and put their canoes or boats in and take them out.

Now, if someone were to take a four -night float trip. Where would they spend the nights?

Well you could start floating at McGuire, and the first day float would probably end at Cherry Hill. The area there has quite a bit of open ground around, and it would just be rough camping. There are no facilities. The second day you would float to Pine Ridge, from there to Oden the third day, and the fourth day down to where 270 crosses the Ouachita at Rocky Shoals.

So they'd be going into the lake at that stage of the game?

Well, then you've got two more days to go to the lake. You could go from Rocky Shoals to Dragover or River Bluffs, which is 12 miles, and then stay overnight and finish up the trip on the bottom part of the river as it enters into the lake at Highway 27. It's possible to float a good six days.

What about the person that only wants to canoe for maybe four hours? Is that available here on the Ouachita?

We have short trips. During our warm weather, like July and August, we have what we call our mini floats, which is just a four- mile stretch of water and it takes about two hours. This is cheaper than our regular floats, but most people like it because it's just two hours of floating time and they don't get worn out. You get awful hot on the water, and so they will float the four miles in two or three hours. For fishermen, four miles is enough to spend a good five hours fishing.

What about fishing on the Ouachita?

The Ouachita is one of the better smallmouth bass streams in the country. It's ranked about even with the Caddo River in that respect. It's a bigger river than the Caddo and floatable longer. The Caddo has a tendency to dry up and get pretty low and you're walking more than you're floating, but you can float here all summer long. The smallmouth fishing gets real good about the first of April and will stay good clear up through until the water gets cold in December. The smallmouth is the most popular fish. It's one of the better game fish, more lively.

What do you recommend for lures ,or do you use live bait for fishing on this particular river?

We use both. Some people use only artificial lures, Little Crawdad crank bait and Rooster Tails. These are what they generally will use and prove to be most successful during the season. Purple worms with high tail and the Rapalla minnows, those are the more popular bait as far as artificial lures are concerned. Live bait is good anytime; you can catch crappie on minnows. We use worms and we use crickets. Crickets are good for perch, crappie and bass. Lot of our people use crawdads too–the live crawdads. They'll also use grasshoppers.

What about swimming on the river? Can people swim if they have a canoe?

They can swim whether they have a canoe or not. Chances are that if they have a canoe, then they will swim somewhere along the line. That doesn't mean that everybody that gets in a canoe is going to turn over, but some people, I'd say in the hot weather especially, have a tendency to be in and out of the canoe a lot. As they are out of the canoe, they'll find good places to swim, holes of water where it is plenty deep to swim.

Do people have to be concerned about snakes?

I don't care where you are you ought to be concerned about snakes.The snakes won't bother you if you don't bother them. Water moccasins are a little bit different. But generally you wouldn't need to be concerned about the snakes other than if you go floating. You want to be careful and watch when you're floating underneath trees, limbs and brush and things because they have a tendency in the warm weather to lie along a limb of a tree. If you come along and knock them off, they could drop in the boat. Usually if one of them drops in the boat with me, he can have it because I'm going out.

You've been managing float trips now for quite some time. Have you ever had a serious problem with a snake with one of your people?

Never have. The people come back and say how many snakes they saw. But, that's not unusual. A lot of people will never see a snake. We've never had any problem with snakes other than a few people who are super fearful of them and we tell them to stay away from the brush, trees, and stay in the canoe.

If someone wanted to spend a week, does this area offer a lot for them to do?

The floating on the river could easily occupy a couple of days. If they're hikers, they could spend another couple of days hiking. We do combination trips. We'll organize a trip for them so they can hike for a day. We meet them at the end of the day or the beginning of the next day, put them in the canoe and let them float for a day, and meet them again, and let them hike for a day, alternating. Now they have all kinds of forest service campgrounds that have been developed, four or five of them, going down through Lake Ouachita, starting at Rocky Shoals. They can camp out there if they just want to camp and laze around for a day or two, swim, fish. If it's hunting season, they can even hunt. They can bird watch, bear watch. We have quite a few black bears. We had one just ramble right down the road here the other day. There's a lot to do. This particular area would be ideal for people who wanted to do that kind of thing for a couple of days, and then if they wanted something different, they could go crystal digging at one of the mines here. That's an interesting thing for them to do if they are inclined to be rock hounds at all.

24. TYPES OF FISH

Courtesy of the Arkansas Fish & Game Commission

The following types of fish are found in Lakes Catherine, Hamilton and Ouachita: Blue Catfish, Bluegill, Channel Catfish, Crappie, Flathead Catfish, Hybrid Striper, Largemouth Bass, Rainbow Trout, Redear Sunfish, Spotted Bass, Striped Bass, Walleye and White Bass.

25. FISHING–LAKE OUACHITA

An Interview with James Norman
President of the Ouachita Watch League

What are the major changes you've seen in the lake over your lifetime?

The major change in the lake would be the number of people who are fishing and using the lake for recreation. Seems like the use pattern was stable through the 60's, and then in the 70's really began to increase as more and more people took up fishing. I think tournament fishing was responsible for an increase in interest in black bass. At first I didn't like tournaments at all, but now I'm beginning to think that they may be a good thing for the black bass. They're practicing conservation of the resource through catch and return. They're also promoting the propagation of large-mouth black bass to be stocked in the public waters. Just a general promotion of sporting ethics as well as sponsoring boat limits, length limits and things of that nature. In general making people more aware of the need to conserve.

Actually when you were young, the lake didn't exist did it?

No. The lake filled up in 1953 and 1954. I guess I started fishing the lake with my folks in 1954, right at the very beginning.The lake then was full of little bass that were anxious to jump on anything they saw, very aggressive. One of the things I do remember about the early years of the lake was the tremendous number of bass that came up the rivers and into the smaller streams. I'm sure they were stockers, and I'm sure they came from the lake because the river just had more fish in it than it had ever had for a few years.

Do you find specific species of fish are fished for at different times of the year?That is, what is the seasonal fluctuation?

I suppose one of the first fish–if you're speaking of spring fishing up at the mouth of the headwaters to the lake, up towards 27 north–you would be speaking primarily of walleye, starting about February. Fishing is related to the weather. There is no way around it. If you get a warm spell in February, the fish are going to run toward the tributary streams. If you then subsequently get a cold front come through, they are going back to the deeper water. So timing is half of everything, or 9/10's. The second thing you'd see running would be your white bass and concurrently with them would be stripers. We're talking March now. Late February, or March, depending on weather, rainfall patterns and so forth.

But when they begin to run in these spring months, you're going to find them moving west, so to speak, towards the mouth?

Yes, not all of them. That would be too much of a generality. Many fish will spawn right in that lake where they happen to be. They just move into a depth of water that is suitable. That, of course, will vary according to the water clarity, how far the sunlight will penetrate into the water.

Will you find the fish in clearer water or denser water?

Both. In years past, particularly in the 60's and 70's, after a good warm rain in the springtime, I would head for muddy water or colored water in a minute. I think primarily because the fish reacted to the temperature of the water coming into the lake. More recent years this hasn't proved to be as consistent as it has in the past. I don't know why. But fish are still where you find them. You have these movements toward running water...all species of fish in the springtime.....but some fish will spawn throughout the lake, and that includes white bass, stripers and black bass, the whole nine yards.

Is the fish activity or availability as great in the hot months of the summer as you find in the spring and fall?

The fishing will be generally a little slower through the summer months. It is still available. The patterns are just different.

You'd fish deeper at that point?

Yes, generally speaking, particularly if a thermocline forms in the lake. Not all years, but many times.

10.Tournament fishing on Lake Ouachita

Are specific places better for fishing if the thermocline forms?

Of course. That would take in contour that would correspond to something right around the top of the thermocline. The top of the thermocline may vary from one side of the lake to the other due to wave action, etc. This would definitely cause the fish to mainly use a depth of two to three feet around the thermocline. Good fishing places would include the flats on the lake which are the tops of ridges, which correspond to thermocline depth, or if it's even shallower, where the depth is correct, you should find some fish, particularly if you have good structure. Drop off and brush piles are good structures to fish with.

How does the fishing profile change in the fall?

In the fall the water cools, and the fish tend to move toward shallower water. They don't go back in the pockets and streams like they did in the spring; they may just move up to a shallow area of the flat, which would be the more likely thing. As the weather cools and the water on the top layer cools, then you will get a mixing as the top layer grows more dense and sinks through the thermocline. They call it "the lake turning over." The water will be black. There may be some debris on top. Just hang up your rod for a few days and go jogging. After the thermocline is gone, you just don't know how deep the bass may or may not go or how shallow. If there is a lot of water at the dam, you may have a considerable amount of just homogenized water. The fish may actually wind up feeding better in the fall under certain conditions.

What about fishing at the dam?

I think below the dam you get the stripers due to the cold water. Trout and things of this nature will respond to increased water flow at times they are generating power. Also, possibly some bait fish will pull through the turbines while they are generating, and they may stimulate the stripers and trout to a feeding frenzy.

Can you give me some recommendations on bait?

As for lures, top water surface lures or floating lures work particularly well in the spring and fall. Preferable lures would be a Smithwick Devils Horse, the Smithwick Toothpick, Spook, things of that nature. If you're floating on the streams, things like Hidden Tiny Chugger, Woodchuck, or noisy surface lures seem to work best. Something that I haven't found to be true on Lake Ouachita is spoons working well at this time. However, after two good hard frosts you begin to find the school fish back and vulnerable to the spoon. Worms are one of my favorite summer time lures. Determine if the bass are holding at any particular depth or just below the thermocline, and the thing to do is to work contour on the points and flats mainly. Keep your lure in productive water as long as possible with particular attention to brush piles, moss and things that attract an old bait fish. Live bait I haven't used in a coon's age.

If you were, what would it be?

Worms, crickets, and there is some excellent live-bait fishing in Ouachita. By the way, you'll find the bluegill in the summer to be almost using the exact same area that the large- mouth are occupying. If the largemouth are at 22 feet, you'll probably find the bluegill at 22 feet. Shad is a popular live bait for stripers, particularly in the fall and winter. Of course, minnows are always a favorite for crappie fisherman, although sometimes it seems a jig will work just as well or better.

Is there anything you want to say about weather?

Weather tips: if you can, fish before a front, cool front. Try to avoid fishing behind a strong front if you have the choice. Be aware that we can have violent weather, and the storms to watch,on Lake Ouachita particularly, are those that approach from the northern quadrant, either from the northwest or northeast. If one seems to hang on the horizon, in the same place for a few minutes, I would suggest leaving the lake. I have done so post-haste a time or two and got out just in time for the hail. The storms out of the south are generally not as violent. Storms can approach rapidly, but there is no need to panic. If you're caught out, you are generally close to an island or to the shore. Just seek shelter immediately. You're going to get a little wet, and you might get a little hail on your head.Throw a cushion over your head, but it's no emergency. It is more comfortable to beat these storms and go back to the dock.

26. FISHING—LAKE HAMILTON

An Interview with Jerry Pownell
Owner of 270 West Fisherman's Choice.

I'm interested in different facts about Lake Hamilton. What kind of fish do you have?

Well, we have catfish, white and black bass, stripers, walleye and crappie.

Does that vary from season to season?

Some of your fish are more or less seasonal. Catfish are

slow right now. Crappie are starting to hit, and bass fishing is all year round.

April normally is your best month. Crappie are coming in early this year.

Now when the lake temperature hits 60 degrees, the white bass run up the creeks. The lake temperature right now is 58 degrees, so they're getting ready to run. They catch a few walleye and white bass earlier. But when the lake temperature gets 60 degrees, the whites run up the creeks.

Are there weather conditions you have to be aware of when you're fishing on Lake Hamilton?

Well, normally, on any lake, it's true that after a storm goes through, it will take about two or three days until the lake levels off and until your good fishing starts in again. Now during a rain is excellent fishing.

Tried a lot of night fishing here in this area?

Quite a bit. You use black baits. It's a scientific fact. A study done at the Oklahoma State University for three years proves that the fish eat black better at night. They can see it better, evidently.

What sort of baits do you recommend for night fishing?

There again, depends on the time. Sometimes we're hitting top water lures or shallow runners. Sometimes they go deeper. Again, depends on the weather.

Will those deeper lures be used in the springtime or will that be more a summer phenomenon?

That will be summer and fall. Right now we're using shallow runners, but in April they'll start down a little bit.

Is there anything unique about Lake Hamilton that you don't find on Lake Ouachita?

They have hybrids here. They don't have them on Lake Ouachita. It's the difference in the bottom of the lake. Now they have Kentucky Bass on Ouachita that we don't have on Hamilton because they don't like the bottom of the lake.

What's the bottom of the lake like here?

It's dirt. There's more sand and rock bottom on Lake Ouachita than there is on Hamilton.

What about different types of baits? Do people like to use live baits here?

Some people won't use a plug or artificial bait...others won't use live bait.

What do you see as being the favorite type of artificial bait?

Shallow running plugs. I recommend Cotton Cordell's Boy Howdy. Missouri Spooks, Smithwick plugs are generally looked for. My favorite bait out of the whole business is the Swedish Pimple.

Is that a shallow runner also?

It depends on how you use it. It's a spoon that you can put deep or bring it in shallower. It catches fish.

What about worms?

We sell quite a few worms and night crawlers, depending on what you want to catch. For catfish they use night crawlers mainly. For bream and things they use the worms.

What about purple worms or some of the artificial worms?

Your bass take those. Right now, for April, May and June, they'll be hitting top- water worms or floating worms. This is normally the only time you get to use those. However, the way the weather has been affecting the fishing the last two years, they've been using them in the fall, too. Now in the spring-time you want to use 4-inch worms, nothing over 6 inches. When you get up to October, September and end of August, you can use a 15-inch worm, a great big one. I sell quite a few 15-inch worms then because they won't hardly hit anything under an 8-inch.

What about fly fishing? Does anyone do any fly fishing around here?

There are a few. I had a fly fishing seminar. Windell High out of Glenwood put on a seminar and demonstrated fly fishing and showed people proper technique. He is an expert on it. He has his own TV movies on it. He makes rods and flies and he is a guide on the Caddo River.

What are things that you would want to add about fishing on Lake Hamilton? Are certain ends of the lake better at certain seasons than others?

Yes they are. Right now, when they let the water come out of the dam, it's cold. Matter of fact, the temperature outside along this river up here will drop 10 to 20 degrees. Even in summertime when it's real hot you can tell when they're letting water out because the temperature will drop right away. The air temperature drops when the water's that cold. In cases like that some of your crappie and things like that stay at the other end of the lake. They don't like the colder water. Now when they run the water like that your bass, and things run up the creeks, back in the coves and places. Then the stripers come out. They like that cold water, and they'll set up a picket line around the mouth of that creek waiting on them to come back.

That's a good tip. Do the striper also like to hang around at the bottom of the dam? Would they be fairly deep when they were doing that?

Yes. They are fairly deep up there. Now they balloon fish over there. They'll put a big minnow or shad on a hook, and you bring it out so far and tie a balloon on it and throw it in the water and then follow the balloon.

Do striper take other bait besides shad?

They'll take big brood minnows. Some of your fishermen would just as soon use that. Your guides prefer shad. But some of them, like Charlie Brenner that comes down here every winter from Iowa, he'll come in and buy 3-6 pound of brood minnows from me every week, and he catches 40-50 pounders all the time. A week ago he caught a 41-pound catfish on one fishing for striper.

Do stripers take any artificial bait?

They take plugs. There's some Big Bomber plugs. Certain

times of the year they'll take blue and white plugs like a Rebel, or that one from Cordell, and then they take the Big and Little Macs.

What time of the year would they take those blue and white plugs?

Later on in the spring. And then sometimes in the fall.

You know pretty much what's going on week by week and day by day in terms of water temperature and best baits.

If you want walleye, your best walleye fishing would be straight across from SunBay.Here is Anthony Island. Here's the highway that goes across. Back up here in this big creek, Williams Creek, you go up in here and you troll out over that sandbar. Divers have come up and reported that walleye are stacked up down there like cordwood. I've never had anybody I've told go over there and not catch walleye.

Okay, if you're interested in walleye, that's the place to do it. Any other place in this lake that specific fish like to hang out?

Well, your stripers hang out from 270 where we're located right here north to the dam.Then they'll get around this bay right here going in to Bull Bayou (stripers). Now you get hybrids all along in here. You go back up in the Mazarn and you can find bass, crappie, bream and catfish.

Sounds to me like the best fishing is from SunBay up to you at Hwy. 270 and then up to the Dam.

The south part of Lake Hamilton is good for warm water crappie. Normally in June, the first two weeks, you can follow the crappie right around Kelly Creek here and load your boat. Once again, this is the 270 bridge at Kelly Creek, a very nice part of the lake. I can see it as I go to Mount Ida when the leaves are off the trees. It's a wonderful part of the river to live on, I think. The only thing is if you come back in here, you gotta be careful. I can walk all the way across there and never get my shoulders wet. You've got shoals on the right-hand side there. You've got to stay more to the center of the left as you're coming up Kelly Creek.

If you want to know about Catherine, there's one worm
that works excellent on Catherine, better there than it does
the other lakes, and it's called a Camellia. It looks like an ugly
old brown worm, and when you hold it up to the light it turns
a brilliant purple. You throw it in the shadows and when it
comes out in the sunlight, the bass hit it.

Ouachita. It's one of the most beautiful lakes there
is—good fishing and especially now in the summertime fishermen would rather go to Ouachita because of the traffic.
TheChamber of Commerce and everybody promotes playing
on Lake Hamilton, but they don't promote the fishing. You
get a lot of skiers, speed boats and things like that, and you
have to watch yourself.

11.View of Lake Hamilton from SunBay

So the fishermen are going to be happiest on Ouachita. Someone that wants to parasail, jet ski, water ski, all that will do better down on Lake Hamilton.

Well, they do it on the Ouachita too, but it's not as prevalent as this here.

Any other thoughts you have on these three lakes?

People think it might be silly but one good thing to do if you are going fishing is to look at the daily paper at the moon phase and see when the majors are and when the minors are. When it's time for the major, two hours before to two hours after will be your best fishing during the day. On a minor period, one hour before and one hour after. Don't ask me how it works, but it does. Even in animals, when it comes to that major, the dogs are up eating, trotting around doing everything. When it's out, they're lying down. Cattle will do the same thing. If the moon can affect the ocean and tide, it can affect the fish and everything that lives in it.

You have a lot of bait, everything that the fisherman needs here. You've got lake maps and a free cup of coffee. Thank you, Jerry.

27. WATER SPORTS

a. Swimming

State Parks (no fee)
DeGray,Lake Catherine,Lake Ouachita

Ouachita National Forest (use fee)
Albert Pike, Charlton, Crystal, Dragover, River Bluff & Rocky Shoals Float Camps.

Corps of Engineers Lake Areas (no fee)
Although the following areas are mostly campgrounds, those listed do have a swimming area for day use. It may or may not be in the camping area, and there is no fee.
Brady Mountain, Buckville, Crystal Springs, Denby Point, Highway 27, Joplin, Spillway, and Twin Creek. (See map of Lake Ouachita for locations.)

Rivers
The Caddo River has good swimming at the narrows at Caddo Gap. The Ouachita River has swimming at each of its listed float camps (see map on back cover.)

b. Scuba Diving

Lake Ouachita is noted for its geological formations and thus attracts many scuba divers. Dive shops can be found at Mountain Harbor and Brady Mountain on Lake Ouachita. In Hot Springs, Scuba & Archery Center is highly recommended.

c. Jet Skis and Wet Bikes

Jet skis or wet bikes can be rented at Lake Hamilton Resort & Conference Centre(767-5511) and Taylor's Water Toy's(525-4146),or purchased at Red River Marine(767-2511) and Cycle World(623-2483).

d. Marinas

State Parks

DeGray(865-4501), Lake Catherine (844-4176), Lake Ouachita(767-9366).

Lake Ouachita

Brady Mountain, (767-3422) Crystal Springs (991-3361), Denby Point,(867-3651) Highway 27 (867-2211, Mountain Harbor (867-2611 or 867-2191), Little Fir (867-3335), Shangri-La (867-2011), Spillway (767-2997).

Lake Hamilton-

Milligen Bradford Marina (767-3376), Holiday Harbor Marina (525-1386), Hot Springs Boat Club & Marina (525-4466), Taylor's Water Toys(525-4146) Other marine suppliers: Red River Marine(767-2511) and Trader Bill's Outdoor Sports(623-8403).

Lake Catherine-

Diamond Head (262-9924)

A B C'S

OF THE

AREA

28. ACCOMMODATIONS

by Dr. Pat Jordan

Great variety exists in your choice of places to stay in the Ouachitas! Almost all the accommodations you may choose are informal (casual dress) and family oriented. It is possible to spend a two-week vacation and never wear a tie or suit jacket AND be accepted at every attraction or function you wish to enjoy.

On the other hand, if you enjoy fancy dressing, the race season at Oaklawn offers certain areas such as the Jockey Club, where minks and diamonds abound.(See the section on Oaklawn Race-Track.)Several of our larger hotels also provide a place to "see and be seen"! *NEVER* let the word "resort" put you off. Generally, these offer a delightful restaurant and great scenery!

Resorts & Hotels

The "rule of thumb" for resorts is *TRY THEM!* The <u>biggest problem</u> for the visitor is that these wonderful places are easy to reach but often nestled away and not directly on the beaten path! *I* have made great mistakes in avoiding resorts because they were six miles off the main highway. I was tired and hungry and didn't know what I would find at the end of the road. What a mistake! At the end of the road is usually a comfortable, often rustic, restaurant overlooking water with good food.

Many people think of a resort as very fancy and upscale. Some are, and these will be highlighted. But the majority of resorts around the lakes are comfortable and relaxed. Generally, resorts on Lake Ouachita will be quieter, more rustic and "farther from the beaten path", while those on Lake Hamilton will be "more glitzy" and surrounded by the attractions city living offers. Typically, resorts have motel rooms or cabins, a restaurant (do try Shangri– La's pies), pool, marina and boat docks.

Driving west toward Montgomery County and Mt. Ida, you will pass several resorts. Brady Mountain is considered by many to be an extremely pretty part of the lake. Brady Mountain Resort has guest rooms, a restaurant, marina, rental boats and a sightseeing cruiser. Crystal Springs is under new management:Tommy and Nancy Trantham are your hosts. All buildings were totally remodeled, including the motel ,lodge, cabins and restaurant. New houseboat, party barge and cruiser docks were built, along with a full-service marina. All rooms are air-conditioned and the restaurant, Kin Fokes, is very nice. Shangri-La and Denby Point Resorts are much closer to Mt. Ida. Shangri–La has a wide variety of accommodations, from cottages that sleep 8 people to double rooms. Locals enjoy the steaks and pies in their restaurant. Denby Point, on the west side of the inlet, has apartments as well as rooms, a gift shop, a conference room for family reunions or seminars, and a full-service marina with new covered slip space. (**See Back Cover**).

The largest of these lakeside resorts is Mountain Harbor. In a class by itself, it hosts world-class fishing tournaments and offers luxurious amenities while preserving a rustic atmosphere. From its 900- slip marina to the rental of bass boats, ski boats and party barges, its water facilities are unequaled. Accommodations range from standard rooms to luxury condominiums complete with jacuzzis. They invite you to stay for a night or become permanent residents! You can buy properties from their residential sales office, Neighbors of Harbor. Although Mountain Harbor offers the complete facilities of a large resort, its environment and atmosphere are relaxed and simple. The Lodge, their restaurant, offers roaring fire on crisp evenings.! It's worthwhile for you to enjoy a meal at one of the resort lodges even if you are staying elsewhere. The views are beautiful, and the food is different than you will find along the roadside, yet not overly expensive.

Within the metropolitan Hot Springs area you will also find resorts. They will also be on the water—in this case Lake Hamilton–with beautiful views and all the amenities. However, they will be more likely to have night-time entertainment and big-city flair. Resorts offer watersports, swimming, fishing and much more. Those on Lake Hamilton cater to parasailing, jetskiing and waterskiing more-so than Lake Ouachita which prides itself on fishing. Lake Hamilton has a number of resorts,some large, some small. Ask for the amenities available when you call for information or reservations.

The lower portion of Lake Hamilton lies south of the Hot Springs Mall, about a 15-minute drive from downtown. Sun-Bay is a resort, time–share, condominium complex located right on Hwy.7 and the water. It is new,modern and tastefully rustic. The Hot Springs Athletic Club on their grounds is a comprehensive facility with racquet ball, spa, sauna, exercise and weight training programs. Their excellent restaurant and night club make entertainment "close to home." If you are considering locating in Hot Springs, this is an important community to visit.

North on Hwy. 7 is downtown Hot Springs. While there are no "water resorts'" here, three major resort/hotels can be found within blocks of one another, on or near Bathhouse Row. The Arlington has been long known for its spa facilities and its "sister hotel,"The Majestic, has been recently renovated and reflects an aura of bygone elegance. The Park Hilton, at the other end of Bathhouse Row, has covered walkways to the convention center, which is just steps away, and boasts sophisticated conference facilities.

To the west you can find resorts on Hwy 70 (Airport Road) and Hwy 270 (Albert Pike), the road to Mt. Ida. This distinction is important because the two areas are separated by several miles. Check a map of the lake to get a good perspective and locate yourself in the area you wish. West on 270 is the Lake Hamilton Resort and Conference Centre. Its marvelous architecture is perched above the lake, featuring a heated indoor atrium pool with a sauna, Jacuzzi and exercise room. Outdoors you will find jogging and nature trails, a boat dock and a private beach. Jet ski rental is available. Across the street is the Cajun Boilers, a wonderful seafood restaurant, and close by, the Mid-America complex.

If your budget allows, resorts are a delightful base from which to enjoy the area. On the other hand, if you are camping or choosing accommodations more in keeping with a smaller budget, try eating at a resort and staying for a swim or a hike.

Hotels in the city of Hot Springs have the air of grandeur associated with buildings of the era of the first half of this century. The clean lines of the newer Hilton contrast to the stately older Arlington and Majestic Hotels, but the flavor of the hot baths in each of these accommodations strikes a note of times-gone-by when elegance and pampering were the order of the day.

Located on or near Bathhouse Row, the hotels are ideally situated to enjoy the variety of downtown attractions on foot. A leisurely stroll down the magnolia-lined row leads into flower lined footpaths and steaming springs. (See Hiking.) It is also convenient to many tourist attractions and shopping. In the center of Bathhouse Row is the Fordyce Visitors Center for the Hot Springs National Park. It features informative programs on all areas in the park as well as its history. Notice the Buckstaff Bathhouse, the only original bathhouse still used for hot baths.

Local crafts and quartz crystal are just steps away and in many cases are displayed in hotel shops. The Arlington Hotel has a covered Artisans Mall of boutiques and shops, ideal for browsing in rainy weather. Even if you don't stay in a hotel, try to eat a meal, sample the baths or enjoy a hotel shop. It's definitely worthwhile.

A final note! Rates for most accommodations vary during the year. During Race Meet (February thru mid- April) prices may be higher. Many hotels and resorts offer accommodation packages in conjunction with the Oaklawn Racetrack. Be sure to ask about availability. Hot Springs supports a family atmosphere. Thus, family packages and group rates may be very attractive during the remainder of the year.

Resort & Hotel Listings

Downtown Area
Arlington Resort Hotel & Spa- 623-7771
Majestic Hotel & Baths-623-5511
Park Hilton-623-6600

Come Play
In Our Lake

Lake Ouachita

Imagine for a minute the peace and relaxation of a lushly wooded landscape, the pampered luxury of choice accommodations from deluxe rooms, suites or rustic cabins to our comfortable and beautifully appointed condominiums.

Experience an unlimited choice of recreational activities—tennis, swimming, boating, diving and some of the best fishing in the world.

Make it happen at Mountain Harbor! Close enough for a weekend, yet special enough for a whole vacation!

Personal custom service is our specialty. Complete meeting and banquet facilities, a great restaurant, airstrip with pick-up service and full-service marina.

Only 30 minutes from Hot Springs and Oaklawn thorough-bred racing.

Mountain Harbor Resort and Condominiums,
P. O. Box 807, Mount Ida, AR 71957 501-867-2191
Out of state Watts – 800-832-2276

Hot Springs/Lake Hamilton

Buena Vista Resort- 525-1321
The Eagles Rest Villa-767-8338
Edgewater Resort-67-3311
Emerald Isle Condominiums- 525-3696
Hamilton Harbor Condominiums-767-8300
Hideaway Resort-525-8386
Lake Hamilton Resort & Conference Centre-1-800-426-3184
Paradise Point Resort-767-9251
Patton's Lake Resort-525-1678
Shorecrest Resort-25-8113
South Shore Lake Resort-525-8200
Summit Lake Resort-525-1162
SunBay Resort & Condominiums- 525-4691
Wharf Condominiums-525-4605
Willow Beach Lakefront Condominiums-525-4398
Willow Beach Resort-525-1362

Lake Ouachita

Brady Mtn. Resort- Royal, 767-3422
Crystal Springs-Royal, 991-3361
Denby Point- Hwy 270 W., 867-3651
Shangri-La-Hwy.270 W., 867-2011
Spillway Resort-Mt.Pine, 767-2997
Mountain Harbor Resort & Condominiums 270 W.,
867-2191, (800) 832-2276

Motels

Motels of all types and sizes can be found in Hot Springs. Some downtown motels have many of the features of the larger hotels, including thermal baths. Motels on the water may resemble resorts. The Downtowner Motel, which has thermal waters, and the Ramada Inn are located on the north end of Bathhouse Row. At the intersection of Central & Grand, about five blocks south, is another group of motels: the Avanelle, the Hill-Wheatley and Red Carpet Inn. Further south on Central are a number of motels in close proximity to Oaklawn Race Track; two Best Westerns, the Stagecoach & the Sands, the Royal Vista, Anthony Inn, the Fountain Motel, and El Rancho. Many more motels may be found five miles south on Lake Hamilton. Motels in this area will generally have the telephone prefix 525-.

Motels outside of Hot Springs and surrounding Lake Ouachita are likely to be more rustic but are nearer fishing and boating access for that lake. They are also closer to crystal digging if that is your interest. The Royal Oak Motel in Mt. Ida and the Angler Motel in Crystal Springs have pools. The Royal Oak has some rooms with water beds. The Colonial Center is a self-contained environment. They have rooms, a grocery store with great steaks for sale, a service station, a crystal shop, and a mine. Accommodations around Lake Ouachita are somewhat more quiet and remote from the city. They also fill up quickly on fishing tournament weekends or Quartz Crystal Festival weekends.

Lake Ouachita has two motels on the water, one at each end of the lake. Spillway Landing is located four miles west of Hot Springs and then eight miles northwest on Hwy. 227. It has kitchenettes, boat rental,covered docks and a restaurant. At the other end of the lake on Hwy. 27 north is the Highway 27 Fishing Village. Popular with locals and Arkansans who want to get away from it all, it has no T.V. They do offer cabins, dock rental and a restaurant.

Most motels in downtown Hot Springs offer color cable T.V., air-conditioning, restaurants and a pool. Prices range from $20.00 to $50.00 per night for a double. Check with the individual motel for particular amenities.

Motel Listings

Downtown Area
Avanelle Motor Lodge- 321-1332
Anthony Inn-623-1102
Apple Tree- 624-4672
Bellair Motel- 624-9244
Best Motel- 624-5736
Best Western Hot Springs Inn- 624-4436
Best Western Sands Motel- 624-1258
Best Western Stagecoach- 624-2531
Capri Motel- 623-1668
Cottage Court Motel- 624-9674
Cove Plaza Motel- 624-7791
Days Inn-624-3321
Downtowner Motor Inn & Bath- 624-5521
El Rancho Motel-624-1273
Fountain Motel-24-1262
Happy Hollow Motel- 321-2230
Hill Wheatley Inn-624-4441
Holiday Motel-624-9317
Ina Motel-624-9164
Lynwood Motel- 623-8951

Margarete Motel-624-9745
McKenzie Motel-624-5546
Ozark Courts-321-2817
Park Avenue Motel- 623-4623
Parkway Avenue Motel-624-2551
Perry Plaza Motel- 623-9814
Ramada Inn Towers- 623-3311
Red Carpet Inn- 624-7131
Romer Hotel & Courts-623-6646
Royal Vista Inn-624-5551
Shamrock Motel- 623-1185
Taylor Rosamond Motel- 624-1255
Tower Motel-624-9555
Town House Motel-24-9271
Travelier Motor Lodge-624-4681

Hot Springs/Lake Hamilton
Anthony Island Motel-525-8208
Hamilton Inn-525-5666

Hamilton Oaks Inn-525-5800
Holiday Inn Lake Hamilton- 525-1391
Knollwood Lodge-767-9231
La Casa Inn Motel-525-1660
Sunset Lodge-767-3411
Super 8 Motel-525-0188
Vagabond Motel- 525-8842

Lake Ouachita/Mt. Ida
Angler Motel- Crystal Springs, 991-3334
Aqua Motel-Mt. Ida, 867-2123
Colonial Center-Joplin, 867-2431
Hwy. 27 Fishing Village-Mt. Ida, 867-2211
Lake Ouachita Inn-Mt. Ida, 867-2643
Mt. Ida Motel-Mt. Ida, 867-3456
Royal Oak Inn-Mt. Ida, 867-2169

Bed & Breakfast

More and more people are gravitating to the atmosphere that bed and breakfast establishments provide. Those listed have antique decorations and serve either a continental or full breakfast. The Golden Eagle Sanctuary on Park Avenue north on Bathhouse Row has a decidedly "metaphysical" flavor. They combine antiques, vegetarian meals and crystal chambers for a one–of–a–kind experience. Golden Eagle also houses a Wholistic Center and offers seminars in New Age, healing and American Indian practices.

Listings
Dogwood Manor-906 Malvern,624-0896
Golden Eagle Sanctuary-833 Park,623-4846
Williams House-420 Quapaw, 624-4275
Megan-Lorien House-426 Spring, 624-3926
Stillmeadow Farm-Rt.1 Box 434-D, 525-9994
Vintage Comfort Inn- 303 Quapaw,623-3258

Condominiums

The Hot Springs community consists of many people who wish property ownership on a smaller scale. Some wish year-round living, while others only choose to spend certain seasons in the area. Because of this interest combined with the spectacular scenery, the community boasts several condominium ownership opportunities. Hot Springs Village, SunBay and Mountain Harbor are three located in widely separated parts of Garland and Montgomery Counties. Check the listings above or the yellow pages for others and their locations.

29. ARCHAEOLOGY & ANTHROPOLOGY

The Ouachita Mountain area is rich in history. The following are accounts of several historical events which are subject to speculation, but leave the visitor with much to see and ponder on. The various Indian cultures described below were located primarily between Norman and Glenwood. Visit the area and enjoy its history. While you are there, note the statue in Caddo Gap which marks the furthest westward exploration of the Spanish explorer, DeSoto.

Just over the border in Oklahoma, about 40 miles from Mena, is the Runestone State Park. It is speculated that Viking exploration took place here before Columbus landed in America. The runestone is a large rock inscribed with runic writing and is one of five in the area. The Vikings may have given rise to tales of "white Indian tribes" in the area. Fact or fiction, these tales enrich the area and may enrich your adventures.

Indians In Montgomery County

Excerpted from <u>Montgomery County *Our Heritage*</u>
Compiled by Mary Beth Jackson

The Arkansas Archaeological Society in 1976 published a booklet entitled <u>An Introduction to Caddo Gap.</u> The booklet stated that very little archaeological research in the Ouachita Mountain region has been published and most of what has been documented was produced before 1940. However, unpublished reports, private collections and Arkansas Archaeological Survey records indicate the region has been occupied for many thousand of years.

In the booklet in the section entitled "History of Archaeological Work in the Ouachita Mountain Region" Ann Early of Arkadelphia stated that Paleo - Indian cultures inhabited portions of Arkansas before 8000 B.C. No definite archaeological site has yet been verified in the Ouachita Mountain region, but surface collections from the upper Caddo and Ouachita Rivers have included a few fluted points of lanceolate shaped spears. It is likely they inhabited this area then.

Beginning around 8000 B.C. and lasting perhaps until 300 B.C., the Archaic cultures of hunters and gatherers who used stemmed dart points, notched river pebbles, ground axes, and a variety of chipped stone artifacts identified as knives, scrapers and drills flourished in this area, according to Ann Early.

Dr. John Thomas Greer's "Essay of the Caddo River Watershed" (1985) stated that the first settlers of the Caddo region in the Archaic Period dated from 900 to 1000 B.C. In the 1920s S.D. and S.P. Dickinson found a type of chipped, double-bladed axe, typical of the Fourche Maline culture of approximately 100-800 B.C. This find was made at Buttermilk Springs in the area of Collier Creek. However, V.L. Huddleston dated the site of Brushy Creek in the 1920s at

1000 B.C. to the first century A.D. and identified it as part of the Marksville Culture. Huddleston said that culture was followed by Cole's Creek culture, characterized by its pottery and mound burial technique with the corpse in a flexed position.

Schambach, according to Ann Early, stated that after 300 B.C. the character of the material culture of peoples living in southwest Arkansas changed. Thick undecorated pottery with bone and later with clay tempering was manufactured. New styles of dart points and chipped stone tools appeared, and some new artifact forms were found—such as chipped stone 'axes' and 'spades', boatstones, and clay pipes. The general term for these cultural manifestations is Fourche Maline. The evidence accumulated so far indicates that the mountain region was occupied by substantial numbers of people, and that new systems of social organization and making a living most likely were developed. These systems differed from the previous Archaic life styles. Quarrying of novaculite and argillite along the upper Caddo and Ouachita drainages for the manufacture of the tools continued (Bond, 1971).

Ann Early stated that at some time between 800 and 1000 A.D., a new cultural complex developed, representing a way of life based upon the cultivation of corn and other domestic plants. These societies and socio-political beliefs included the construction and maintenance of ceremonial centers containing temple and burial mounds. These centers did not appear to have been villages, or compact communities. The population was, instead, dispersed along river and creek valleys in small hamlets or farmstead residential sites. New styles of pottery were made , and engraved and incised decorations on finely made, highly polished pottery bowls, jars, and bottles became common. Tiny, finely flaked arrow points have been found in sites, indicating that people were using bows and arrows for hunting and warfare.

12. *Statue commemorating DeSoto's furthest westward movement.*

However, Ann Early continued, the date of the first Caddo occupation of the Ouachita Mountain regions is unknown. A single phase of occupation has been identified, on the basis of the appearance of certain types of pottery vessels and clay pipes, which has been given the name Mid-Ouachita. The principal component of the Adair site, some thirty miles northeast of Caddo Gap, was that of a Mid-Ouachita phase ceremonial center.

Dr. J.T. Greer stated in his essay that Tom Collier's discoveries in 1925 and Dickinson's excavations in 1927 established a new culture in this area in 1400. Shell-tempered pottery was found by Dickinson along Collier Creek and Buttermilk Springs. However, some evidence exists which could suggest that this group of Indians was not of the ten tribes of the three-group confederation known as the Caddo. Prior to DeSoto, however, the inhabitants of the region believed that they had "received the title of the land from the gods" (Lyons: 1952). The name Caddo is derived from French "Cadodaquois" of the eighteenth century and refers to the "Great Chiefs" of the Kadohodacho, the Caddo Indians, who may not have come into the valley proper until the late 1700s (Greer). This differs from the findings of Dr. Swanton, from the Smithsonian, along with Colonel John R. Fordyce on the DeSoto Commission in 1939, who thought the Tula Indians to be Caddo Indians. (In 1541, DeSoto referred to the Indians in the area of the Caddo Gap region as Tulas.)

DE SOTO

Historians still do not completely accept the fact that Caddo Gap was the site of the historic meeting of DeSoto and the Tula Indians. The DeSoto Commission, formed in 1939, studied the four narratives about DeSoto's stay in Arkansas. All speak of DeSoto's stay at the" hot streams" at a place named Tanico, and of a battle with the Tula Indians a short way (three days' march by the entire army) to the west/southwest. The DeSoto Commission felt that Tanico must be the area of the present-day Hot Springs, and that the Tula Indians encountered by DeSoto were in Caddo Gap..." "Assuming that Tanico was near the present town of Hot Springs—and there are no other sizable hot springs in this vicinity—a trail upstream but to the southwest would probably have led up Big Mazarn Creek to the Caddo River just below Caddo Gap. Here the Caddo breaks through a narrow opening in the novaculite stone ridge, and on the up-stream side the valley widens out and there are many signs of an Indian village including several mounds. This was probably the site of Tula."

Today the statue in Caddo Gap commemorating DeSoto's 1541 visit and the mascot of Caddo Hills School District—the Indian–are lasting memorials to the first inhabitants of Montgomery County. Students on the Caddo Hills campus and amateur and professional archaeologists continue to find artifacts and evidence of early Indian villages up and down the Caddo River Valley.

Indian Burial Ground in Norman

An Interview with Duane Cox, Mayor
By Dr. Pat Jordan

Currently, one of the most unique Indian findings has involved the city of Norman and its mayor, Duane Cox, in a major shift of direction. This shift reflects a commitment to preservation and restoration of the historical heritage of the area.

Norman had finally decided on the location of their waste-treatment facility. Bids had been let, contracts signed and the bulldozer work begun on leveling the site. As part of his activities one afternoon in September of 1988, the mayor was at the site checking on the work in progress. As he looked down at the ground where the bulldozer had just moved earth, he found what appeared to be a human femur. His immediate fear was that he had found an unsolved homicide. Within the hour, a local physician had confirmed that they had, in fact, unearthed a human bone.

Archaeologists confirmed the next day that the remains were Indian and quickly had the site placed on the National Register. Bodies, vases and arrowheads were found. It was a burial site–located one and a half blocks from City Hall at the intersection of Huddleston Creek and the Caddo River. Archaeologists, Ann Early, Hester Davis and Martha Rolingson, became involved with the project. They felt it was a very important site and speculated that the remains and artifacts indicated the burial ground had been in use from four hundred to four thousand years.

Burial grounds are exciting history, but the mayor had a waste-treatment plant scheduled for completion, and the plans were already set in motion. This is a dilemma which has plagued the remains of Shakespeare in England and many Indian sites in this country. I do not wish to minimize the political considerations that must have gone into the final decision to find a new site for the waste-treatment plant. It is a credit to Norman and its mayor that from that day on, no bulldozing was done at the site, and construction was halted immediately.

The unearthed graves were re-interred with proper ceremony performed by American Indians from Oklahoma. Future plans for the site may include a building which will house replicas of both artifacts and structures found in the area. This will be accomplished if funds and interest allow.

The Heavener Runestone

Courtesy of the Oklahoma Tourism & Recreation Department
by Gloria Stewart Farley

The Heavener Runestone was first discovered, according to local oral history by a Choctaw hunting party in the 1830s. Poteau Mountain, on which it is located, was named by French trappers. It was part of the Indian Territory ceded to the Choctaw Nation when they were removed from Mississippi to present Oklahoma. The Choctaws were probably astonished if they saw the eight mysterious symbols punched into the mossy face of the huge slab of stone which stood in a lovely ravine, protected by overhanging cliffs.

Although there is no test to determine the antiquity of an inscription on stone, such as the C-14 test on organic matter, the weathering of the edges of carving in relation to the hardness of the stone and the exposure to the elements is an acceptable guide. The site of the Heavener Runestone is in a deep ravine, protected from wind on three sides. The stone itself, twelve feet high, ten feet wide and 16 inches thick, is in a vertical position and thus is protected from ice erosion.

Three geologists confirm that it fell eons ago into its north-south alignment. There it stood like a billboard, waiting for someone to write on the broad west face. The fine-grained Savanna sandstone is, to quote Dr. W. E. Ham, former state geologist, "so tough that it can be broken by a geologist's hammer only with considerable difficulty." The eight runes are in a straight line, six to nine inches in height, and still one-fourth to three-sixteenths of an inch in depth. Weathering is so slow, that a date written in lead pencil on the flat gray lichen on the stone, exposed to rain and snow, was still legible seven years later. And yet the edges of the runes are smooth and rounded by weathering.

For sixteen years, the mystery of what the runes meant had been diligently pursued. Scholars here and abroad had been stumped because the runes were from two ancient runic alphabets, as agreed upon by three foremost runologists and the Smithsonian Institute. These were: six of the runes are from the oldest Germanic (Old Norse) Futhark, which came into use about 800 A.D. A runologist from Norway transliterated the runes as: G N O M E D A L, and suggested that it might be a modern name, G. Nomedal. However, to do this, he had to consider that the second rune was unfinished and the last rune was reversed. Two other runologists said it made no sense and had to be a modern fake. None of the three had seen the Heavener Runestone, so apparently they had not realized the labor required to carve the runes into the very hard stone, nor had they considered the weathering of the inscription.

In 1967, a new translation was offered by Alf Monge, former U.S. Army cryptographer, who was born in Norway. Refusing to alter the shape of the Heavener runes, he said the correct transliteration is G A O M E D A T. The letters will not translate into sense, he stated, because they are used not as letters, but as numbers, according to their places in two alphabets. Then by using a cryptographic method, which had been invented by ancient Norse clergymen to hide dates in runic inscriptions, based on the positions of numbers in calendars and Easter Table, he said the Heavener inscription is also a Norse cryptopuzzle, hiding the date of November 11, 1012, St. Martin's Day. He explained that the use of the two alphabets was deliberate and necessary to give the month, the day and the year.

Although the cryptopuzzle is a complicated process and not accepted by all scholars, at present it appears to be the most feasible translation yet offered. The date does fit into the time frame of history as written in the ancient Norse sagas. They record a colony was attempted on the New England coast about 1008 A.D. Two years later, the colony failed, two ships returned to Greenland and one sank. There is no direct record of the fourth ship. Some modern Norse historians believe it to be possible that the colonists had already explored south to Florida. And their fourth ship, instead of returning to Greenland, then explored the Gulf of Mexico, ascended the Mississippi and thus found its way via the Arkansas and Poteau Rivers to the site of the Heavener Runestone by the year 1012.

The authenticity of the Heavener Runestone was further enhanced in 1967, when two thirteen-year-old boys found another inscription ten miles away on a hill at Poteau. The eight symbols were also from the same two runic alphabets but included a rare numerical symbol used in the ancient Norse Easter Table and a variant rune. Alf Monge stated that the Poteau Runestone inscription hides the date of November 11, 1017, exactly five years later than the date of the Heavener Runestone, and that the maker of both could be identified as the same person. Originally part of a ledge, the broken-off Poteau Runestone is exhibited at the Kerr Museum near Poteau.

In 1969, another small stone carved with five symbols from the oldest runic alphabet was found face down near Shawnee, Oklahoma and interpreted by Monge to be another Norse cryptopuzzle with the hidden date of November 24, 1024. It is also displayed at the Kerr Museum.

30. ARTS

Hot Springs

In the last couple of years, Hot Springs has attracted a vital and active artist community; it has been called the "Santa Fe" of the new decade. Paint, pots, metal and cellulose are just the bare outlines of the media utilized for creative expression. What animates the arts in Hot Springs is its spirit! It is not isolated; it is connective. It is not local; it is international.

The art community has spearheaded an energy which not only draws new talent to the area but involves the community on a inter-active basis. The excitement which this segment of Hot Springs generates can be seen and felt as you walk on Bathhouse Row and on down Central. Notice that some buildings with sad remnants of a glamorous past still exist. Then look at the lively restoration of their neighbors as you enjoy the treasures of more than twenty galleries.

The Cafe New Orleans is located across from Bathhouse Row. Its artistic flavor supports poetry readings and a wide variety of entertainment which the public may enjoy.

Montgomery County

Art in Montgomery County focuses on the performing arts. The Montgomery County Council for the Performing Arts has blended the best of local talent with new residents, and the mix has yielded fresh energy and ideas. This cooperation has given birth in the past five years to musicals such as "Oliver," "Sound of Music," and "Fiddler on the Roof". The group draws from the entire county and supports casts as large as fifty players ranging in age from three to eighty years.

Musicals are the spring event, drama for the fall. Musical revues, the "Messiah", and a variety of dinner theaters make up the offerings for the rest of the year. In the summer, the MCCPA sponsors a performing arts workshop at Camp Ozark for as many as sixty elementary-aged students.

Gallery Walk

Hot Springs has a delightful new tradition the first Thursday of every month! It is the Gallery Walk. From 5 PM.to 9 P.M., a broad range of galleries remain open and offer special exhibits, often featuring the artist, music, refreshments, and lively conversation. If you are in Hot Springs at the beginning of the month, experience this gala event. Dress is casual and admission free!

31. ATTRACTIONS

Hot Springs has such a diversity of attractions for the visitor. As if its water and mountainous scenery weren't enough, it offers a wide variety of things to enjoy. Choose to tour the city on the White or Yellow Ducks which drive through town and straight into Lake Hamilton, or take a romantic carriage-ride around the city or sail Lake Hamilton on the Belle of Hot Springs. From sightseeing to luncheon cruises to sunset dinner/dance cruises, you're sure to enjoy the excitement and beauty of Lake Hamilton. Several musical shows are performed in Hot Springs: Music Mountain Jamboree, The Bathhouse Review and Rocky Top Jubilee. Natural attractions include: Ar-scenic Spring, Hot Springs Mountain Tower, Mountain Valley Water,and the splendor of Gulpha Gorge and the National Park

Be sure to walk north on Bathhouse Row to the intersection of Park and Whittington. Up Whittington are several tourist attractions which should not be overlooked. The Dryden Pottery, the Educated Animal Zoo and the Arkansas Alligator Farm are all located on Whittington. Some may want to drive to these attractions.

Below are listed several of Hot Springs'/Montgomery Co. Attractions. You will find many more listings under **Kids—Fun For The Younger Set.** Also, look for the brochure "Top Family Attractions" at the Visitor's Center.

AR-SCENIC SPRING - 307 Mt. Ida St., 623-1722. The oldest commercial business in Hot Springs.

BASKET HOUSE- 4620 Central Ave., 525-2652. This attraction features the Southland's largest selection of native and imported baskets, Arkansas whetstones, Ozark apple dolls and local pottery. See an original Hot Springs "turn-of-the-century-trolley" on the premises.

BATHHOUSE SHOW - 701 Central, 623-1415. Family–style music & comedy revue.

BELLE OF HOT SPRINGS - 6205 Central, 525-4438. 400 passenger riverboat,sightseeing,lunch & dinner/dance cruises.

CANOEING - Floating the Ouachita River for two hours or two days is possible in Mt. Ida at Ouachita Heights(326-4710) or Ouachita Joe's(325-5517). Enjoy the Caddo River with Wright Way (356-2055) or Arrowhead (356-2944).

CRYSTAL MINING- Crystal mining may be enjoyed close to Hot Springs at Coleman's mines or in Mt. Ida. See the **Crystal**

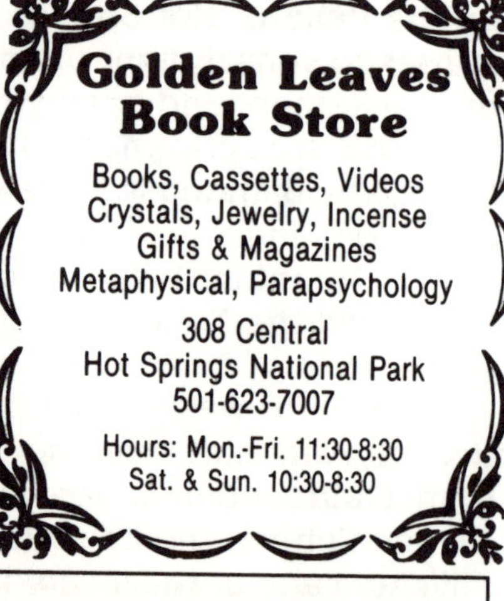

One of the Largest
Selections of Books
On Crystals
Native American
Environmental Issues
Available in Arkansas

section for locations.

HOT SPRINGS MOUNTAIN TOWER- Atop Hot Springs Mountain is a tower with an awesome view of the Ouachita Mountains and the National Park, 623-6035.

JOSEPHINE TUSSAUD WAX MUSEUM - 250 Central , 623-5836.

MOUNTAIN VALLEY WATER - 150 Central , 623-6671. Tour the restored headquarters for free.

MUSIC MOUNTAIN JAMBOREE - 270 W. at 3300 Albert Pike, 767-3841. Night time stage show of family fun & music.

ROCKY TOP JUBILEE - 1312 Central, 623-7504. Hot Springs' newest family gospel/country music show.

TAYLOR'S WATER TOYS- 6201 Central 525-4146. Parasailing, wet bikes, jet skis, and more! Every type of water fun.

THE WHITE AND YELLOW DUCKS-The amphibious "Ducks" leave downtown and travel out Hwy.7 south where they float Lake Hamilton.

THE WITNESS - 623-9781. The greatest story ever told is portrayed in this outdoor drama. Weekends at Mid-America.

32. BOAT RAMPS

Paved ramps
Avant
Avery Day Use Area
Big Fir
Brady Mountain
Buckville
Lena Landing
Crystal Springs
Denby Point
Highway 27
Joplin/Mt. Harbor
Lake Ouachita State Park
Little Fir
Spillway Day Use Area
Tompkins Bend/Shangri-La
Twin Creek

Unpaved ramps
Rabbittail
Cedar Fourche

33. CAMPING

Cam grounds and day use areas fall under the jurisdiction of several different government bodies. The areas in Hot Springs and Montgomery County are listed here under the appropriate heading. Addresses for the agency with responsibility for the site is listed. Contact these agencies for information and maps (free).

Army Corps of Engineers
The following campgrounds are maintained by the Army Corps of Engineers. The Corps' offices are located at P.O. Box 4, Mountain Pine, AR 71956 (767-2101). Their offices are

next to Blakely Dam, and it is worth a visit if you wish lake information. Note Lake Ouachita map for campground locations.

Avant–0 units
Avery Day Use Area– 0
Big Fir– 17
Brady Mountain– electric, showers, 72
Buckville–5
Cedar Fourche–0
Crystal Springs–electric, showers, 61
Denby Point– electric, showers, 67
Highway 27– electric, 10
Irons Fork–5
Joplin/Mt. Harbor– showers, 65
Lake Ouachita State Park–electric, showers, 102
Lena Landing–10
Little Fir– electric, 25
Rabbittail–0
Spillway Day Use Area
    Stephens Park– electric, 9 units
Tompkins Bend/Shangri-La–electric, showers, 77
Twin Creek– 15

Forest Service

For information related to use of Forest Service lands, please contact the following:
Ouachita National Forest
P.O. Box 1270
Hot Springs, AR 71902 (321-5202)
    or
Womble Ranger District
P.O. Box 255
Mt. Ida, AR 71957 (867-2101) On U.S. 270, Mt. Ida.

Charlton– showers, 69 units.
Clearfork–Group area, 8 cabins, showers.
Collier Spring–Picnic area, 3 units.
Crystal–9 units.

Float Campgrounds:
    River Bluff– 7 units, no fee.
    Fulton Branch–7 units, no fee.
    Rocky Shoals– 7 units, no fee.
Gap Creek– Roadside picnic area, no fee.
Hickory Nut Mountain– 8, no fee.
Lake Ouachita Vista– Scenic View of Lake Ouachita.

State Parks

Information of State Parks can be obtained from:
Arkansas State Parks
1 Capitol Mall, 4A-900
Little Rock, AR 72201 (501-682-1191)

Lake Ouachita State Park–electric, showers,102 units, swimming, cabins, marina, and Three Sisters cold springs.

National Park Service

More information is available from:
Hot Springs National Park
P.O. Box 1860
Hot Springs, AR 71902 (501-624-3383)

Gulpha Gorge – 47 units, toilets, no electric or showers. This beautiful site is located right in Hot Springs.

34. CARS: Street-Rods & Hot-Rods

Old cars, whether they are restored, customized or street-rods, are a popular interest for many families today. Throughout Arkansas you can find activities which involve some form of automotive fun every weekend. They are open to the public and family oriented.

In downtown Hot Springs, visit the Reed Museum of Automobiles at 714 Central Ave.(321-1166). They display classic antique cars seven days a week for a small fee. There is also an antique car museum at Petit Jean State Park(see listing on State Parks).

Street-Rod events are held almost every weekend within a two-hour drive of Hot Springs. You will find about one hundred cars in variously wonderful stages of renewal. If you want a leisurely stroll through a lovely park or quaint main-street area with the added pleasure of looking at old cars, contact one of the representatives below. They are affiliated with the Arkansas Street Rod Association and will be happy to give you all the information you could want on every aspect of automotive fun in the Ouachitas.

There are two drag strips in the area: Centerville located north of Hot Springs near Russellville and Prescott Raceway south on I-30 . Each is located about one and a quarter hours from Hot Springs. Prescott races on Saturday evening, and Centerville races on Sunday afternoon. They have paved strips, but the spectator and pit areas are more like picnic grounds; in fact, many do barbecue. Very family oriented.

Oak Grove Raceway is a circle track located between Mt.Ida and Glenwood which races every Saturday night weather permitting. If you are in the Mena area, there is a circle track located at Cove, AR, just south on Rt.71.

Sprint car racing is featured every Saturday night at the I-30 raceway in Benton just west of Little Rock. For information on all auto events call:

Hot Springs-Buddy McGriff,767-6290
Glenwood-Max Whisenant,356-3634
Mt. Ida-Bill Ray,867-3666, 867-2749

35. CHAMBERS OF COMMERCE

The Chamber of Commerce is a great place to get information on most places of interest in an area. They will have free pamphlets on camping, attractions, restaurants, parks & recreation and much more. Here are several area Chamber numbers for your benefit.

Mt. Ida-867-2723
Greater Hot Springs-321-1700
Mena/Polk county-394-2912
Glenwood City Hall-356-3613
Murfreesboro/Pike County-285-3131
Hot Springs County-332-2721

36. CHURCHES

Please call the Chamber of Commerce number or Municipal number listed above for church information. This part of the country has many churches, and a major part of community activities centers around the church. Visitors are welcome and residents friendly!

37. CLIMATE

By the Greater Hot Springs Chamber of Commerce
Retirement Development (501-321-1878)

Hot Springs' climate is generally mild enough to allow year-round outdoor activity. The summers are long and warm and the winters short and mild. Spring and fall are extremely pleasant. The irregular topography (ranging from 400 to 1000 foot elevations) and abundance of hardwood trees and blooming dogwoods make the spring and fall outdoor colors spectacular.

The annual rainfall is 55 inches, and the skies are generally clear or partly cloudy more than 200 days each year. The annual expected snowfall is only three inches, and freezing temperatures might occur for a period of less than 50 days.The average relative humidity of 55 percent and general wind speed of 8.1 miles per hour add to the pleasant climate.

AVERAGE TEMPERATURE	High	Low
January	52	31
February	57	34
March	65	41
April	75	52
May	82	59
June	89	67
July	93	71
August	93	70
September	87	63
October	77	53
November	63	42
December	55	35

38. DAY TRIPS

Information taken from Arkansas State Parks Brochures

Crater of Diamonds State Park

Situated among the pine forests of southwest Arkansas near Murfreesboro is a rare 40-acre field where diamonds can be found in their natural matrix. Over 70,000 diamonds have been found at the "Crater." Other semi-precious gems and minerals can also be found: amethyst, agate, jasper, quartz, calcite, barite and many others.Take U.S. 70 south to Rt. 27 south to Rt. 301. Phone: 285-3113.

Crystal Loop

This 13-mile swing through the crystal and cold springs country of Montgomery County is described in the **Crystal** section.

De Gray State Park

This fine state park is just 21 miles south of Hot Springs on on Rt.7. It encompasses an island lodge and convention center, camping, a 132 -slip, full-service marina and picnicking. An 18-hole championship golf course is open to the public; fishing is excellent for pros and beginners alike, and sailboats, jet skis, and water skiing abound on the lake. For information & reservations contact: De Gray Lake Resort State Park, Rt.3, Box 490, Bismark, AR (865-4501).

Lake Catherine State Park

Situated just 15 miles from Hot Springs, Lake Catherine State Park has a year-round lodge, camping, park restaurant, fishing and water sports, and boat and canoe rental. Contact: Lake Catherine State Park, Rt. 19 Box 360, Hot Springs, AR 71913-8605 (844-4176).

Little Missouri Falls

This is scenery not to be missed. Directions and description in the **Crystal** section.

Petit Jean State Park

Petit Jean State Park lies in a unique area between the Ozark and Ouachita mountain ranges. In this lovely mountain setting are an abundance of unmarred woods, ravines, streams, springs, spectacular views and interesting geological formations preserved almost as French explorers found them 300 years ago. Its stunning beauty is punctuated by a waterfall and rock house cave.

The mountain received its name from the legend of Petit Jean, a French girl who disguised herself as a boy and secretly accompanied her sweetheart, a sailor,to America. Its facilities include a lodge, cabins, camping, restaurant, picnicking, fishing, canoeing, swimming, hiking and tennis. The park may be reached by taking Hwy. 7 north to Centerville and then Hwy. 154 east to the park.

Queen Wilhelmina State Park

Situated along Talimena Scenic Drive in western Arkansas, just 13 miles west of Mena on Rt. 88, this park is the jewel in the crown of the park system. The park is perched atop Rich Mountain nearly 3,000 feet above sea level. The scenery and lodge feel like Volcanoes National Park over looking Kilauea volcano in Hawaii.

The lodge with 38 rooms is open year-round. The dining room has a good buffet, and in the summer a fast food window is open. Camping with electricity and water is available. The kids will enjoy miniature golf, an animal "petting park" and a miniature railroad–big enough for adults.

While you are in the vicinity, consider driving the 54 -mile Talimena Scenic Drive. It offers breathtaking vistas and includes information stations at each end of the drive–Mena in Arkansas and Talihina in Oklahoma. Historical sites along the route reveal a past when early settlers and the Choctaw tribe in Indian Territory struggled to wrest a life from the harsh land. The park's address is: Queen Wilhelmina State Park,Rt. 7 Box 53 A, Mena, AR 71953 (394-2863 or 2864).

Toltec Mounds Archaeological State Park

Toltec Mounds are the remains of a large group of ancient Indian earthworks. Identification of the site with the Toltecs is a mistake. Although the original owner of the land believed the mounds to be of Mexican origin, investigations by archaeologists proved these mounds had been built by ancestors of the American Indians.

The culture which built the Toltec Mounds is named Plum Bayou. The people lived in permanent villages and hamlets where they farmed, gathered food, fished and hunted. This center had a population primarily of political and religious leaders and was built from about 700 to 950 A.D. To reach Toltec Mounds take I-30 to I-440 to U.S.165 to Rt.386 which leads into the site. Excavation is in progress.

13. Juanita Johnson of Pencil Bluff sells modern quilts in traditional styles.

39. FESTIVALS & FAIRS

Craft Fairs

Arkansas is famous for its crafts and craft fairs–and well it should be! Some of the biggest and best-attended craft fairs in the U.S. are held in the state. Fairs feature quilting, weaving, wood-working, baskets, and more creativity than you can imagine. You can find a craft fair almost any and every weekend of the year. Sharon Heidingsfelder, P.O. Box 391, Little Rock AR 72203 (671-2000) is the state coordinator for the Arkansas Cooperative Extension Service. She can give you current listings from the "Directory of Craft Fairs in

Arkansas." Below are listed several festivals and fairs in the Hot Springs/Montgomery County area.

Caddo Springfest

The Springfest is a two day festival which includes canoe races–both single and double-as well as dancing, music and the usual crafts. It is held in Norman the last weekend in March.

Arkansas Arts & Crafts

Hot Springs in March.

Charlie Weaver Day

The last Saturday in April is the celebration of Charlie Weaver Day. He made Mt. Ida famous with his Mama's letters from Mt. Ida. Stroll the square, enjoying crafts and music.

Mountain Fest

Sponsored by the Ouachita Arts and Crafts Guild, this fair is held in Mena in mid-May.

Lum'n'Abner Day

Held in Mena in June, this fair celebrates the famous ole' time radio-show hosts.

Mena Quilt Show

Held in Mena in June.

Good Old Summertime

Hot Springs in July.

Good Neighbor Days

Held on Labor Day in Norman, this fair is free to all and serves up a great meal of barbecue and all the fixin's. All the residents turn out for this fair. Music, gun-swaps, crafts and more. Go early. The food's usually gone by noon!

Caddo Sawmill Days

Glenwood highlights the days of logging that are so much a part of the heritage of the area. Crafts, music and an antique car show. End of September.

Oktoberfest

This four-day celebration is the grandaddy of Hot Springs' festivals. The convention center serves up Oom-Pah-Pah in every manner possible: German food, polka music and crafts. Craft enthusiasts should note that this weekend is the nationally acclaimed War Eagle craft show in the Ozarks so there will be fewer exhibitors at this time. Entertainment abounds, and most restaurants and businesses celebrate. October.

Quartz,Craftz & Quiltz

Held at the Montgomery County fair grounds in Mt. Ida, this festival features a three-day quartz crystal dig with prizes for the finest specimens, fun digs for the kids, music and performances by the MCCPA. The three main buildings at the fair grounds feature quartz for sale, crafts for sale, and quilts for sale. Third weekend in October.

Mena Arts & Crafts Fair

Mena in October.

Garland County Arts & Crafts Fair

This is Hot Springs' premier craft show with more than 350 exhibitors. October.

Hot Springs Holiday Craft

Hot Springs' Christmas crafts show makes for good gift and decoration buying. December.

40. GOLF

When the subject of golf comes up, most people lament the lack of courses in the Hot Springs area. However, for the dedicated, some <u>do</u> exist, although a couple are approximately an hour and one-half drive away. Ah, the price of duffing! In Hot Springs, let me mention two private courses that you must be a guest of a member to use. This is not to tantalize you, but you may be considering moving to the area or could have friends with memberships. These are Hot Springs Village(four courses) and Hot Springs Country Club. Belvedere Country Club is private, <u>but</u> it is possible to use the course.

The following are public eighteen-hole golf courses:

1. In Bismark, about 20 miles south of Hot Springs on Rt. 7 is the De Gray Golf Course in De Gray State Park.

2. Heading west on Rt.270, you can turn left at Rt.88 and travel to Mena (approx. 70 miles). In the city itself is the Lion's Club golf course, which is public.

3. On Rt.88 a couple of miles east of Mena, you will find the Ouachita Country Club, which is also open to the public.

4. To get to the Waldron Country Club, as you travel west on 270, pass the turn to Mena and continue on to Y-City. Turn right on Rt.71 and continue on to Waldron (approx.25 miles) where you will find the Waldron Country Club.

There are two nine-hole courses in the Hot Springs area. The first is Lakeside golf course off of Malvern in Hot Springs. The second is located on the grounds of Mt.Ida Footwear in Mt. Ida. A nice addition to the benefits of the plant, the course is open to the public and minimal fees charged.

41. HIKING

Information courtesy of the Hot Springs National Park

Hot Springs National Park has many trails which take from ten minutes to several hours to walk. Information on all of the trails is included and should be used in conjunction with the park brochure. If you plan a long walk in isolated places, consult the Park Service for recommendations on clothing and precautions. Water, for example, is always a good thing to carry. For those who wish a guided walk, inquire at the Fordyce Visitor Center for times when these walks leave.

Please note that the trails are grouped into two sections. While walking the trails, look for the different types of rock outcroppings. These geologic formations were uplifted millions of years ago and are now exposed by erosion in some areas. The most predominant type of rock in the park is novaculite. The area is home to many birds. Nearly 150 species occur within Hot Springs National Park. Look for the mockingbird, the state bird of Arkansas. One of the most visible features of the park is the dense forest cover. The predominant trees are the shortleaf pine, oaks and hickories.

Trails on Hot Springs, North, and Indian Mountains

Fountain Trail - 0.1 mi. - This short access trail begins on Fountain Street between the Grand Promenade and the one-way road going up Hot Springs Mountain. The trail is uphill and intersects with the Honeysuckle Trail.

Arlington Trail - 0.1 mi. - This access trail, for patrons of the Arlington Hotel, connects with the lower loop of the Dogwood Trail.

Tufa Terrace Trail - 0.2 mi. - You can find this trail just off the Grand Promenade at the steps above the display springs or on Arlington lawn to the right of Desoto Rock. Over eons of time, a large volume of rock has formed as a result of the flowing hot waters. Massive terraces of tufa are just below the Grand Promenade overlook. You can also see one of the hot springs flowing from the hillside above the Arlington lawn.

Short Cut Trail - 0.2 mi. - In days gone by, horse-drawn carriages had to follow the road to get to the top of Hot Springs mountain, but those on horseback used this route as a cutoff. The trail angles off from Dead Chief Trail, climbs steeply, and ends at the picnic area on top of Hot Springs Mountain.

Reserve Trail - 0.3 mi. - This easy trail follows the base of Hot Springs Mountain. It begins on Reserve Ave. at the intersection with Dead Chief Trail.

Floral Trail - 0.4 mi. - The trail is a connection between the Dogwood (lower loop) Trail and the Honeysuckle Trail. The entrance is on Fountain Street beyond the Happy Hollow Spring. The trail is uphill both ways. This trail is a good one for wildflowers.

Grand Promenade - 0.5 mi. - A pleasant walk along a wide brick surface. The Promenade extends from Reserve Avenue to Fountain Street and runs behind Bathhouse Row. There are many interesting features to be seen along this walk. The

Promenade was completed in 1957. This is an easy stroll in a landscaped setting. This red & yellow brick walkway behind Bathhouse Row was completed in 1957 and connects Fountain & Reserve Streets. Numerous benches are provided along the walk. Several trails can be reached from the Promenade.

Peak Trail - 0.5 mi. - This trail begins at a point about midway along the Grand promenade and climbs steeply to the crest of Hot Springs mountain. There it joins the Hot Springs Mountain trail.

Honeysuckle Trail - 0.5 mi. - Honeysuckle, a local name for Azalea, was once abundant along this trail but has disappeared. The trail is on the northwest slope of Hot Springs Mountain extending from the one-way road up the mountain to an intersection with the Hot Springs Mountain Trail. The Honeysuckle trail crosses the Peak trail and intersects with the Fountain and Floral trails.

Indian Mountain Trail - 0.7 mi. - A rocky, steep trail up the side of Indian Mountain to a historic novaculite quarry. The trailhead is across the highway from the upper end of the campground. Note the cross walk printed on Gulpha Gorge Road. Be careful when crossing the road.

Gulpha Gorge Trail - 0.8 mi. - The trail begins at a point near the campground amphitheater, crosses Gulpha Creek and then climbs the steep slope of Hot Springs Mountain and North Mountain. Along the way, you can see massive overturned beds of Hot Springs sandstone and Arkansas novaculite. The trail intersects with two other trails - Dead Chief and Goat Rock.

Goat Rock Trail - 0.9 mi. - The trailhead is on the right just before you reach the overlook on North Mountain. Goat Rock is a massive pinnacle of novaculite .7 mile from the trailhead. The trail intersects with the Gulpha Gorge Trail. Two miles beyond Goat Rock and is moderate walking except for the climb up to Goat Rock itself, which is 400 feet up off the main trail.

Dead Chief Trail - 1.43 mi. (walk time: 1 1/2 hours-The trailhead is just off the Grand Promenade above the display springs area. The first part of the trail is steep; then it levels off and follows along the base of Hot Springs Mountain where it intersects with the Gulpha Gorge Trail, .2 mi. from the campground. This is the easiest walking route between the Bathhouse area and the campground, a total distance of 1.6 miles.

Hot Springs Mountain Trail - 1.7 mi. - The trai-head is just across the road from the lower end of the picnic area on top of Hot Springs Mountain. It is a level walking loop trail and encircles the mountain just below the crest. You may see several small brooks along this trail if drought has not dried them up. There are also many examples of exposed novaculite outcroppings.

Dogwood Trail - 1.9 mi. - This trail is thickly dotted with dogwood trees. The glistening white understory of blooming dogwood climaxes the spring flowering season. There are two loops to this trail, an upper and a lower. The upper loop trailhead is just below the overlook on North Mountain, and for the most part the walking is easy. Access to the lower loop is from the Arlington Trail. From that point the walking is not difficult, but it is all uphill.

Trails Beginning on West Mountain

Canyon Trail - 0.7 mi. - The trailhead is just across the road from the picnic area on the West Mountain Summit Drive. From here, the trail descends steeply along the north side of West Mountain. Along the lower end, the trail follows the route of an old carriage road. From the top, the walking is easy. The lower end of the trail ends at Canyon Street.

Oak Trail - 0.9 mi. - This trail extends from an intersection with the West Mountain Trail and follows along the south slope of West Mountain. Many large oak trees, both white oaks and red oaks, can be seen along this trail, intermingled with the shortleaf pines and hickories.

Whittington Park Trail - 1.1 mi. - An easy walking trail in a pleasant urban setting with gravel trails(west section recreation/exercise trail).

West Mountain Trail - 1.2 mi. (walking time: 1 1/2 hrs.) - The trailhead is near the picnic area on the West Mountain Summit Drive. Here you are near the midpoint of the trail, which extends westward along both the north & south sides of the mountain. Each leg of the trail intersects the mountain-top trail. Using a segment of that trail, you can make a loop which takes about an hour. For the most part the walking is easy.

Mountain Top Trail - 1.4 mi. - This trail extends from Whittington Avenue to Prospect Avenue over the top of West Mountain. It is a steep, strenuous hike going up, but an easy descent. The trail crosses Sunset Trail at a point .2 mile from the end of the West Mountain Summit Drive.

Sunset Trail - 8.5 mi. - The trailhead is at the West Mountain Summit Drive. This is a rough trail over natural surface, both level and with some climbing. This is the longest single trail in the park. The route generally follows the ridge line and ends at Blowout Mountain on the northern most boundary of the park. During the hike, you will pass Music Mountain, the highest point in the park, and the trail to Balanced Rock, a rock pinnacle with an outstanding view and Indian Quarry site (novaculite). Dress comfortably, wear your favorite walking shoes and carry water. NOTE: The National Park has a handout which gives greater detail of the Sunset Trail and its various sections. Ask for it.

U.S. Army Corps of Engineers Trails

The Woodpecker Hollow and Buckskin Nature Trails are each one–half mile loops. Each has a booklet that explains marked points of interest along the way. These two trails begin at Denby Point Campground and are worthwhile for the novice hiker. Another trail of interest is not for the hiker. The Army Corps supervises the Ouachita Geo–Float trail. This is a marvelous trail of geological wonders that can be viewed from the water by boat.(**See Stanley's Fold**.)

U.S. Forest Service

The Womble Trail winds through Montgomery County for 29 miles. It begins on Rt.27 north of Mt. Ida where the Ouachita River bridge crosses the highway. Look for the sign. It also can be picked up at a number of float camps along the river. This trail generally follows the river. For more information on this trail, stop at the Womble Ranger station located just east of Mt. Ida on Hwy.270.

14. Hiking near Brushy Recreation Area north of Pencil Bluff.

42. HOSPITALS

In the unlikely event that you are hurt, there are two hospitals in the Hot Springs area. AMI National Park Medical Center's phone # is 321-1000. It is located at 3110 Malvern Road. St. Joseph's Regional Health Center's phone# is 624-5451 and it is located at 100 Whittington Avenue.

There are two hospitals in the area that specialize in specific therapies. For those who suffer from arthritis, the Levi Arthritis Hospital is highly respected nationally(#624-1281). The Libby Memorial Physical Medicine Center uses the thermal waters in various treatments for therapy (#321-9664.)

Ambulance and EMT service is available in Montgomery County by calling 867-4211 or 867-3151. The number in the Norman area is 334-2400. An air ambulance is available. The Sheriff's Office in Mt. Ida can be reached at 867-3151.

43. HOT SPRINGS NATIONAL PARK

Information Provided by the Hot Springs National Park

Hot Springs National Park is different from all other National Parks. That's because it's the oldest area in the National Park System. Originally called Hot Springs Reservation, it was declared to be an area set aside for all the people in the United States in 1832. Although there were other places in the East that had hot springs, the Appalachians for example, these were the only springs in the central part of the country. Springs, hot or cold, were important because they were used medicinally in those times. Doctors would recommend different spas for different illnesses.

Many people came to Hot Springs with rheumatism or arthritis. Quickly the Springs' reputation grew as a cure for various ailments. Bathhouses were built, and soon a town grew with hotels and boarding houses for travelers to stay in while "taking the waters." This is why Hot Springs National Park is the only park located in the middle of a city.

One of the bathhouses has been renovated and today is the home of the Fordyce Bathhouse Visitor Center. Located in the middle of Bathhouse Row in downtown Hot Springs, it is easily seen on the south side of the park's old carriage entrance which is marked by bronze eagles atop limestone pylons. Its ornate copper and glass marquee will also catch your eye as you look for this three-story tan brick building.

The Fordyce Bathhouse was built in 1915 to be "the most practical, complete, and luxurious Bathhouse in the world." It operated until 1962. By that time, modern medicines and transportation were carrying visitors to other vacation spots. With fewer bathers coming, the bathhouses in town experienced a decline in business that caused many to close from 1962 to 1985.

After it went out of business, the Fordyce Bathhouse was purchased by the National Park Service and designated as a tour building to be converted into the park Visitor Center. Opened on May 13, 1989, the Fordyce Bathhouse Visitor Center offers a glimpse of the "Golden Age of Bathing" during 1915-1923 in Hot Springs. You can tour the ground floor on your own, view the park's introductory movie, the historic bathing area, and browse in the bookstore.

Flora and Fauna

Forestation characterizes the flora of the park. The northern slopes of the ridges and basins provide a suitable habitat for deciduous forest dominated by oak and hickory. Pines predominate on the south sides of the ridges. Other shrubs and trees that flourish in this environment include yaupon, eastern hackberry, elm, juniper, dogwood, serviceberry, redbud, and holly. Ground cover in the spring and summer includes pinks, verbenas, phlox, spiderworts, golden ragwort, purple cornflower, rose gentians, asters, butterfly milkweed, and sunflowers. These species are a few of the various wildflowers found in the area.

A wide variety of animals have lived in the park area over the centuries. Bison, wapiti, mountain lion, and wolf left the region after the arrival of European and American settlers. Some of the present-day species near the hot springs include squirrel, rabbit, opossum, fox, coyote, skunk, raccoon, gopher, weasel, mink, rat, frog, and armadillo. Hot Springs National Park lands lie in the Mississippi flyway, which means migratory birds, game birds, and waterfowl spend portions of the year in the park vicinity.

Hot and humid weather characterizes the climate during the late spring and summer months, with occasional periods of drought occurring during late summer. Long falls, mild winters, and early springs with few frosts and snows mark the seasonal progress of the year. This climate produced a typical southeastern woodland environment conducive to exploitation by aboriginal people.

15. Downtown Hot Springs

44. HOT SPRINGS AFTER DARK

Let me begin with a comment about the Ouachitas, excluding Hot Springs. After dark there is little to do outside of your campground, resort or personal circle of friends. The counties which make up the Ouachitas are dry, so there is no dancing or drinking to speak of. Except for Mountain Harbor and possibly other resorts on the weekends, the majority of restaurants close at 7 P.M. or 8 P.M. There is one movie theater in Mena. Since you are surrounded by gorgeous scenery, you are probably tired from a day filled with activity.

BUT for those who wish to "party hearty," Hot Springs awaits. The following places have music—either disco or live entertainment on the weekend. Entertainment during the week is sporadic. Call ahead.

Acapulco Restaurant–band, 623-8030
Coy's, T-Bird Lounge– disco all week, 321-1414
Dad's—Ramada Inn-band, 623-3311
Fat Dave's Lounge—band, 525-3584
Illusions (new multi-level club)—band, 623-5072
Sawmill Lounge—one-man band, 623-3082
Shakey Jake's—R.&R. disco, 525-5675
Sock-Hop—Holiday Inn, disco, 525-1391
Teddy Baer's—Lake Hamilton, band, 767-5511
Windows on the Bay—SunBay, band, 525-4691

45. INSECTS

Ticks

I remember well my first experience in "tick country" on Cape Cod years ago. They seemed to be everywhere, and they made my skin crawl! This section is written to calm your fears and simultaneously sharpen your awareness.

First, in polling the doctors in Mt. Ida, they have only seen two confirmed cases of Lyme Disease. They also see very little Rocky Mountain Spotted Fever. Tularemia, or rabbit fever, is seen more often but still is not a frequent occurrence. It is important to be aware of the symptoms so that if any do occur after you have left the area, you can see your doctor. Be sure to mention that you have been in a tick locale. The diseases caused by ticks can be diagnosed by a blood test.

Lyme disease is spread by the injection of spirochetes into the body. However, a tick will generally crawl on the body for several hours before it decides to settle on you as a meal–and an inferior one to it's way of thinking! After it bites you there is a period of (according to the individual researcher) two to twenty-four hours before the infecting agent is injected. A local doctor's office explained that the tick must eat and become full of blood before it injects the spirochetes. Therefore, you have a fairly long period of time to notice the tick and remove it.

There are many ideas on how to remove ticks, but the latest strategy is–do it quickly. This is because the mouth parts which bite you do not harbor spirochetes. The Forest Service Health & Safety Code Handbook advises,"Remove any ticks that have become attached. Do this with your fingers or tweezers. Grasp the tick as close as possible to the point of attachment and pull gently and repeatedly. Treat the bite and wound with antiseptic and wash your hands thoroughly with soap and water. NOTE: do not try to burn the tick or cover it with heavy oils."

It is recommended you check the bite occasionally for at least two weeks to see if a rash forms. If one does, seek treatment. Other symptoms may include profound tiredness, stiff neck, headache and flu-like symptoms. Other tick diseases may have rapid onset with high fever and chills along with severe weakness. In Rocky Mountain Spotted Fever a rash will develop about four days after the bite. It usually starts on the hands and extends to most of the body.

The Forest Service Handbook recommends that you wear clothing that fits tightly at the ankles, waist and wrists. Each outer garment should overlap the one above it. Cover trouser legs with high socks or boots and tuck shirttails inside trousers. Light-colored clothing helps in seeing crawling ticks. Search the body repeatedly, especially hairy regions and inside clothing, as ticks seldom attach themselves within the first few hours. Make a practice of examining children and pets before bed. Always wear tickrepellant when you walk in the woods. If you develop symptoms even several months after being bitten, do not fail to tell your doctor that you have possibly been bitten by a tick.

Chiggers

Chiggers seem so simple and harmless in comparison to ticks–until you are itching out of your mind and would trade the entire experience for a single tickbite. Chiggers are almost microscopic and usually reside in long, damp grass. They leave bumps from the size of a pin to the size of pennies–depending on your sensitivity and the degree of scratching. Oh, how they itch!

If you are bitten, take a hot bath and lather up several times. This kills the chigger, but the welt will still itch. Recommended home remedies are alcohol wiped over the area on a regular basis for the first several days, or meat tenderizer rubbed onto the bites. Clorox is also recommended. Alcohol seems to work wonders on both chigger and tick bites for me. Remember, an ounce of prevention is worth a pound of cure. Use insect repellant and layer clothing as you would for ticks.

Spiders

Two spiders reside in the state that are worth mentioning. Tarantulas are often seen on the road in the evening enjoying the remaining heat. They are a problem only if you are walking. Although they are large, they are generally docile and easily avoided. Children in the area bring them to school.

The brown recluse is also present in the state. It is, as its name indicates, reclusive. You are likely to find them in dark, unused places. Their bite in most cases is not fatal but can be very painful, with total atrophy of the tissue surrounding the bite. It is best to seek medical advice if you believe you have been bitten.

46. KIDS-Fun for the Younger Set

Hot Springs and the Ouachitas are family oriented. It would be hard to find many activities that the kids wouldn't enjoy. The following list gives suggestions for activities that are traditionally oriented toward the younger set.

Aquarium
Located at 209 Central and part of the National Park, this aquarium boasts Arkansas' largest fish and reptile exhibit.

Go-Karts
There are three places that you can enjoy Go-Karting:
1. Go-Kart Fun (525-8262) is located on Hwy. 7 South on Lake Hamilton just south of Anthony Island.
2. Fun Trackers (767-8140) is a part of Music Mountain Jamboree and is located on Albert Pike just east of the light at Hwy. 227.
3. Ouachita Speedway is just outside of Joplin on Hwy. 270, between Joplin and Hurricane Grove on the way to Mt. Ida.

Horseback Riding
Castleberry Riding Stables has trail rides, hay rides, lessons and more. On Hwy 7 N. to Walnut Grove Rd. (623-6609).

Magic Springs
This amusement park is open June 2 to August 26, plus

selected weekends in April & May, September & October. Located at 2001 Hwy. 70 East (1-800-272-2152 or 624-5411).

Mid-America Museum

A wonderful hands-on museum of practical science. Complete with dinosaur displays, a laser show and a new planetarium exhibit (767-3461). Take Albert Pike to Hwy.227 North.

Mini-Golf

Located in Music Mountain Jamboree Village, Gator Golf, an 18- hole course, may be the most challenging you've ever played (767-8601).

Roller Skating

Crystal Palace Skating Center is at 2002 Higdon Ferry, just south of the Hot Springs Mall. They are open Thursday through Sunday afternoons and evenings. Skate rental is included in the entry price, and Thursday is $1.00 night (525-9927).

Tiny Town

This attraction is located at 374 Whittington Avenue. A town of mechanical miniatures, it is fascinating for all ages (624-4742).

Zoo

Hot Springs has two educated animal attractions. The first, the Educated Animal Zoo, is located at 380 Whittington Ave. They feature an exotic bird show (623-4311). The other is the I.Q. Zoo located at 422 Central (623-7572). These are not to be confused with actual zoos. They have a collection of trained animals (cats, chickens, pigs, etc.) that perform various tricks.

Arkansas Alligator Farm & Petting Zoo is located at 847 Whittington. Petting and feeding the animals are particular attractions.(623-6172)

47. LAKE HAMILTON

Information Provided by SunBay Resort

Lake Hamilton is located on the Ouachita River area nick-named the "Tri-Lakes Region." It has contributed to the cosmopolitan atmosphere that has made the Hot Springs National Park region a world -famous spa.

Lake cruises are offered on the Belle of Hot Springs, a triple deck excursion boat which can also be chartered for dinner or party cruises. Sight-seeing tours of the lake are offered on the Yellow and White Ducks. These amphibious vehicles are boarded downtown, and passengers ride them right into the lake as a guide notes points of interest. Sailing, para sailing, canoeing, kayaking and paddle boating also are popular on the lake, and various small craft can be rented. Spend the day water skiing, scuba diving, or casting a lure for sport fish that vary from a 4-ounce bluegill to a 30-pound striped bass. Spend the evening enjoying some of the best dining and entertainment in the nation.

Arkansas Power and Light cooperates in a fisheries management program for the lake with the Arkansas Game & Fish Commission. It is a cooperative relationship that began in 1939, when AP&L donated 135 acres for the Lake Hamilton Fish Hatchery. The hatchery has more than 90 acres of ponds that contribute some three million fingerlings annually to improve sport fishing. It is one of the most successful sport fish hatcheries in the nation. In fact, Lake Hamilton offers the visitor a smorgasbord of angling oppor-tunities: scrappy redear, green and longear sunfish, black, spotted, white and smallmouth basses, black and white crappie, flathead, blue, channel and bullhead catfish, wall-eye, and chain pickerel. Rainbow trout are stocked as well.

If you want a quiet walk in undisturbed woodlands, an adventurous family can sample its own "deserted island" in Lake Hamilton by exploring Electric Island. This 118-acre island was donated by AP&L to the Arkansas Game and Fish Commission for nongame wildlife management. It is dominated by tall pines and shady groves and is frequented by bald eagles during the winter season. It is located due north of the AG&FC fish hatchery.

See the section on **Waters** for fishing information on Lake Hamilton.

48. LIQUOR

The counties which make up the Ouachita Range and surrounding area are predominantly "dry." That is, they do not serve or sell liquor, beer or wine. This is sometimes in conflict with vacation plans! If you wish to purchase alcohol, the following information will benefit you.

Garland County and the city of Hot Springs are "wet." This means you can purchase beer and wine in the supermarket or beer store, and you can purchase liquor at liquor outlets. Mixed drinks are served with the proper license, and beer and wine are available in many restaurants. HOWEVER, it is not legal to sell such beverages in the State of Arkansas on Sunday unless you have a mixed-drink license. And then the drinks must be consumed on the premises. FURTHER, Sunday begins at midnight on Saturday. So, if you go out for a night on the town, be prepared to stop alcohol consumption at 12 P.M.

Montgomery, Polk, Pike, Hot Springs County (not to be confused with the city of Hot Springs which is in Garland County), Howard, Sevier, Scott, and Clark are "dry." This is not a complete listing, but it covers the counties that border the Ouachitas. It would be wise to buy alcohol either in Garland County or Oklahoma–if you are near that state. From the Mena area, you may buy beer in Oklahoma along routes 4 or 270. However, you must go to Poteau to buy liquor.

A word to the wise! Please note that Arkansas law limits the amount of alcohol you may carry in your car to one case of beer and one gallon of whiskey. Frequently, law enforcement agencies in dry counties will be particularly watchful for liquor law infractions!

49. LUM 'N' ABNER

By Kathryn Stucker, Museum Manager

"Hello, Jot 'Em Down Store. This is "Lum 'N' Abner." That was one of the most welcome greetings on radio for nearly twenty-five years. Chester "Chet" Lauck (Lum Eddards) and Norris "Tuffy" Goff (Abner Peabody) were the creators, actors, writers, sound effects men, directors, and the life of the "Lum and Abner" program. They received more fan mail than any other radio program of the time–1 1/2 million letters one special week!

Their budding careers began as young, amateur performers in Mena, AR., where they grew up together, teaming to entertain at many school and civic functions. On April 26, 1931, representing Polk and Montgomery Counties on station KTHS in Hot Springs, AR., they tried out their old country storekeeper's routine. The names, "Lum Eddards" and Abner Peabody," were a spur of the moment addition and the format was more conversational than situational, but the performers showed so much talent that they were invited back. Then, offered a 13-week contract with NBC and obtaining Quaker Oats as a sponsor, they were off to Chicago for "temporary" show business careers.

Pine Ridge is only slightly smaller now than it was in the early 1900s when it was called Waters, the site of a post office, saw mill, general store, grist mill, blacksmith shop,

16. Lum'N'Abner Jot 'Em Down Store in Pine Ridge.

and the other services necessary to a farm community. Dick Huddleston built his store in 1909 and bought groceries from a wholesaler named Mr. Goff. Mr. Goff's son, Norris, was learning the grocery business, delivering to many Polk and Montgomery County general stores. Mr. Lauck owned the big sawmill in Mena, so all of the residents of this logging country knew his son, Chester, checking the trucks of logs being delivered.

Dick Huddleston was a friend to them all and a leader in the community of Waters. The general store of any small town was its hub of activity, especially on a Saturday afternoon when everyone from the surrounding farms came to town to trade goods and stories. That was the inspiration for the Lum 'N' Abner program. By the mid-1930s the radio program was well-known nation-wide, and the listeners were asking where Pine Ridge was, so the name of the town was changed in an elaborate ceremony on the steps of the State Capitol in Little

Rock in 1936, on the fifth anniversary of the program. Pictures in the LUM 'N' ABNER MUSEUM show all of the participants –the Governor greeting Lum, Abner, and the real-life counterparts of Grandpappy Spears, Cedric Wehunt, Dick Huddleston, etc.

The stores that were so busy on the program are still busy today. They house the LUM 'N' ABNER MUSEUM & JOT 'EM DOWN STORE. The Huddleston Store holds the souvenir and gift shop, and continues to offer Lum 'N' Abner programs and premiums in addition to antiques and crafts. The smaller A.A. McKenzie Store that was built in 1904 and was originally across the street, just as the fictional Jot 'Em Down Store was on the program, has been moved next door and displays the many pieces of Lum 'N' Abner history, preserving an important era in American life.

50. MAPS

Maps of every type can enhance your adventures. Collect them from every agency you visit. Several suggestions are: a Weyerhauser map (free) will give you excellent detail of many of the smaller dirt roads, an Arkansas (AHTD) Highway map (free), and Forest Service maps which can be purchased for one or two dollars at a ranger station. Ask for the free maps at convenience stores in the Mt. Ida area. They may also be available in Hot Springs.

51. MOUNT IDA/MONTGOMERY COUNTY

Evolution of Montgomery County

**Excerpted from <u>Montgomery County *Our Heritage*</u>
by Karen Cosby**

The 487,110 acres that we now call Montgomery County has been known by many names through the years. All of Arkansas was included in the Louisiana Purchase in 1803 when it left French possession and became American property. In 1812 it became a part of the Missouri Territory, and in 1813 Arkansas County was created and included our present Montgomery County.

The Ouachita Mountains were a vast uncharted wilderness when the first white settlers arrived. There were few roads available west of the Mississippi River, and those were merely rough trails. It was a long and often perilous distance from one lonely trading post to the next. From time to time, a restlessness struck a farmer in Tennessee or Georgia, an urge to escape from the increasing population east of the Mississippi. His eyes would turn to the west, that land beyond the Mississippi, so full of space and hope, adventure and danger. Soon, the farmer and his family left the safety of their roads and trails. Once past the Mississippi, their journey slowed as frequent halts were necessary to clear the path for the wagon. The wagon contained a most precious cargo: provisions, tools, seeds, clothing and furniture. All were essentials for a family heading into the wilderness.

Montgomery County was named in honor of General Richard Montgomery, a legendary figure during the Revolutionary War. It was organized under the provisions of an act of the General Assembly of the State of Arkansas which was approved December 9, 1842. In the beginning the county seat was called Montgomery. It was later changed to Mount Ida. In 1850 the name was changed to Salem and six months later was changed back to Mount Ida. The territory was once the hunting grounds for the Caddo Indians and the DeSoto expedition is reputed to have come through the territory in 1543. The first white settlers came up the Ouachita River to the vicinity of Mount Ida about 1836, six years before the county was established.

Montgomery County has 805 square miles of territory, of which sixty-three percent is national forest land. The 1980 census shows 7,771 residents, and,the population has continued to grow. Elevation above sea level at the courthouse is 663 feet. Montgomery County is divided into three school districts: Caddo Hills, Mount Ida and Oden. Montgomery County is agricultural, but the emphasis is changing. Early in the century there were 12,000 acres of cotton under cultivation, now there is none. In cotton's place, beef, dairy cattle, swine, poultry, forest products, mining and tourism have become our most important cash crops. The area attracts many as an excellent place to retire.

Lake Ouachita with its 1,000 miles of fishable shoreline, the Corps of Engineers' many campgrounds, the quartz crystal mines and five modern resorts all add substantially to our economy.

52. NEWSPAPERS

Newspapers in the area:

Akansas Citizen, Hot Springs
Sentinel- Record, Hot Springs
La Villa, Hot Springs Village
Glenwood Herald, Glenwood
Montgomery County News, Mt. Ida

53. OAKLAWN RACETRACK

For the visitor who comes to Hot Springs to enjoy Race Meet, the horse racing season from February to mid-April, Oaklawn needs no introduction. For the visitor who imagines racetracks as seedy and somehow sinister, let me tell you of a place that looks like what you always imagined Ascot in England would look like! Weeping trees and flowers, magnolias and dogwood, manicured lawns and wooded background are the ingredients which make up the visual scenery of Oaklawn. The ambience is one of a steeplechase on an elegant manor.

You may choose outside seating in the grandstand or watch the racing from air-conditioned comfort in a number of increasingly elegant and expensive dining rooms. Oaklawn's latest addition is their Carousel Terrace restaurant, which has individual televisions on each table for personal viewing. The exclusive Jockey Club is a four -level lounge which offers sweeping panoramas of the track as well as monitors. While these clubs are for members only, you can purchase daily memberships for a small fee, space allowing. Minimum admission age is sixteen (ten to fifteen if accompanied by an adult). You must be twenty-one to drink alcoholic beverages and eighteen to bet. During Race Meet purses can be worth up to $500,000.00.

Two welcome innovations were introduced in 1990. The first is Sunday racing, which was voted into effect by the citizens of Hot Springs. The second is the extension of racing season through Labor Day on weekends only. This is done by simulcasting races held elsewhere in the country and allowing betting on the events. This year fans watched and bet on the Kentucky Derby from Oaklawn! It took me three years to get to Oaklawn. However, I have promised myself to go back every season to enjoy one of Hot Springs' most beautiful and exciting attractions! Oaklawn is located on Central Avenue between downtown and the Hot Springs Mall. Its address is P.O. Box 699, Hot Springs National Park, AR 71902 (1-800—RACE OJC)

54. OUACHITA MOUNTAINS

Courtesy of the Hot Springs National Park

Hot Springs National Park is in the Zigzag Mountains, a small range of the Ouachita Mountain system in the interior highlands. The Ouachitas extend from central Arkansas about 220 miles westward into eastern Oklahoma and average 50 miles in width. By studying the relationships of rock and their fossil and mineral contents, and interpreting them in the light of what is happening on the earth's surface today, geologists have pieced together a geological history of this region extending over an immense period of time.

In Paleozoic times, 400 million years ago or more, this area lay beneath the Ouachita Embayment, an arm of a sea which extended from what is now Louisiana to New Hampshire. To the south was a lofty mountain range. Throughout a period of many millions of years, erosive forces wore away those mountains, depositing gravel, sand, mud and chemical precipitates under the shallow waters on the gradually sinking floor of the Ouachita Embayment. These sediments accumulated to a thickness of over 30,000 feet.

Following the long period of deposition, a period of mountain-making forces lifted and compressed sediments, squeezing an area 100 miles wide into a folded, fractured mass just half that wide. These rocks have remained above sea level for more than 200 million years. At least twice, they have been eroded down to low-lying, relatively flat lands known as peneplains, only to be uplifted again and subjected to further erosion. Parts of the peneplains are apparent now as the relatively flat tops of many of the Ouachita Mountain.

Geography And Climate

The Ouachita Mountains are a series of long ridges running east-west across central-west Arkansas. The 1,000 - to 2,700 foot- high ridges are the largest mountains in the central United States. These unique mountains display an overlapping of several different ecozones, resulting in a remarkable array of wildlife and natural vegetation. Northern red oaks can be found along with Southern magnolias. Rich stands of a wide variety of hardwood trees are found on the northern slopes. Southern slopes and valleys are characterized by shortleaf pine, a significant timber source for this region.

Here in central Arkansas, you can enjoy the outdoors throughout the year. The seasons are characterized by four distinct seasons with hot summers and mild winters. During the summer it is best to stay near streams and lakes to enjoy the cool, clear waters flowing from the Ouachita Mountains. The larger lakes maintain comfortable swimming temperatures May through October. During autumn an abundance of hardwood trees creates beautiful arrays of colors across the forest. From October to May you will find beautiful cool weather perfect for hiking, fishing, and hunting. Snowfall usually occurs a few times a year in the Ouachitas, and it adds brief winter beauty to the mountain scenery.

55. PHYSICIANS

If you need a physician in Hot Springs, there are many to choose from in the yellow pages. Two hospitals with emergency rooms are listed in the **Hospitals** section. If you need medical attention in Montgomery county, there are two physicians in Mt. Ida: Dr. Jim Davis (867-2175) and Dr. Helen McClard (867-2105 & 867-2448). Note the EMI and emergency helicopter service listed under Hospitals.

56. RADIO STATIONS

KWXI 670 AM/Glenwood
KBHS 590 AM/Hot Springs
KSPA 96.7 FM/Hot Springs

KZNG 1340 AM/Hot Springs
KQUS US97 FM/Hot Springs
KIXT 1430 AM/Hot Springs
KLAZ 10666 FM/Hot Springs
KGAP 103.1 FM/Hot Springs

57. RESTAURANTS

Restaurants in Hot Springs offer a variety of ethnic cuisine. Mexican, Chinese, Japanese, Cajun, Kosher, Southern Barbecue, Italian, and good old all-American can be found. Fast food such as Wendy's, MacDonalds, and Popeye's are popular for quick eating. Rocky's, across from Oaklawn Race Track, serves a great Italian meal for $3.98.

Resorts around Lake Ouachita tend to serve steaks, fish and chicken and often have buffet-style fare. Restaurants along Hwy. 270 and in Mt. Ida will serve local foods, frequently fried chicken or chicken fried steak and on Friday —catfish. These come with purple hull peas or okra—whatever local vegetables are in season. Mountain Harbor boasts a "home-smoked" barbecue buffet that is a local legend!

Hotel restaurants need to be investigated! Dining can be gala or family-style. Be sure to check out the all-you-can-eat Seafood Feast at the Arlington Hotel on Friday nights. Also, the sandwich shop/soda fountain in the Majestic will take you back in time. Each hotel has its own brand of charm. Try SunBay or the Hilton for brunch on Sunday! If you're looking for an inexpensive home-style lunch, Lake Hamilton Resort & Conference Centre has daily specials for under five dollars.

Several restaurants are award winners. Coy's has won the Arkansas Times Reader's poll for "best steak in the Southwest." La Hacienda is this year's "best Mexican", and Acapulco's,in historicic Lindell Square, won first prize at "Taste of Hot Springs". McClard's barbecue has been written up as one of the outstanding barbecues in the country. Cajun

Boilers has won the Arkansas Times Best Seafood for four years running, including 1990.

The following list is not comprehensive, but it will give you suggestions for a wide variety of eating pleasure.

American
Bonanza- 12 Crawford Dr., 623-3485
Buffy's Buffet- 4605 Central, 525-5793
Club Cafe-1010 Central, 624-9624
Coy's Steak House- Cypress&Reserve, 321-1414**
Downtowner Motel Inn- 135 Central,624-5521
Fountain Motel- 1622 Central, 624-1262
Hamilton House-130 Van Lyle Dr., 525-2727**
Hill Wheatley Motor Inn- Grand & Central, 624-4441
Magee's Cafe- 362 Central, 623-4091
Royale Vista Inn- 2204 Central, 624-5551
Saugatuk- 270 W. On Lake Hamilton, 767-4499
Sawmill Depot- Valley at Market, 623-3082**
South Shore Lake- 201 Hamilton Oaks, 525-4545
Travelier Motor Lodge-1045 E.Grand, 624-4681

American/Kosher
Mollie's- 538 W. Grand, 623-6582 **

Barbecue
McClard's- 505 Albert Pike, 624-9586
Stubby's Hik'ry Pit- 1000 Park, 624-9323**
Stubby's Too- 3024 Central, 624-1552

Cajun/Seafood
Cafe New Orleans- 210 Central, 624-3200
Cajun Boilers- 3506 Albert Pike, 767-5695 **
Country Katfish Inn- 4301 Central, 623-8147

Hotel Restaurants
Arlington Hotel- Central & Fountain, 623-4020
Holiday Inn (Bugatti's)- Hwy.7 S., 525-1391
Lake Hamilton Conference Centre- Hwy 270 W., 767-5511
Majestic Hotel- Park&Central, 623-5511

Park Hilton-1 Convention Plaza, 623-6600
Ramada Inn(Trumpets)- 218 Park, 623-3311
SunBay Resort- 6110 Central, 525-4691

Italian
Agostino's-510 Central,624-5500
Facci's- 2910 Central, 623-9049
Rocky's- 2600 Central, 624-0199
Rod's Pizza Cellar- Spring & Broadway 624-RODS

Mexican
Acapulco-320 Ouachita Ave., 623-8030
El Chico- Hot Springs Mall, 525-4055
La Hacienda- 4716 Central, 525-8203

Oriental
Hunan- 6425 Central (Lake Hamilton), 525-2053
Tsubaki,(Japanese)- 631 Park, 624-9682

Lake Ouachita Restaurants
Brady Mtn.Resort- Royal, 767-3422
Crystal Springs- Royal, 991-3361
Denby Point- Hwy 270 W.,867-3651
Hwy. 27 Fishing Village- 867-2211
The Lodge/Mountain Harbor- 270 W., 867-2191**
Shangri-La- Hwy.270 W., 867-2011
Spillway Resort- Mt.Pine, 767-2997

Mount Ida
Bob's Pizza Shack- 867-2681
Carol's Kitchen- 867-2643
Circle R- 867-2711
Fireside- 867-2273
Mt. Ida Cafe- 867-2283

Other
Belle of Hot Springs- Dinner Cruise 7P.M.
Edelweiss(German)- Spencer's Corner, 624-7866
Hattie's Cafe- Norman,AR, 334-2331 **
Stitt House-Elegant Victorian lunch, 624-5916 **

58. *Retirement*

Retirement is one of the primary reasons for coming to Hot Springs and the Ouachitas. The mild four-season climate lends itself to healthful living and ease of getting around. Winter lasts from late December until late February, but much of this period is characterized by 60-degree sunny days and few nights below freezing. Flowers begin blooming in late January, and the forsythia blooms in February. By the end of March daffodils, tulips and dogwoods are finished or lingering as the magnolias start their showy season.

By May you can expect days in the eighties, and the water beckons. Hot Springs is surrounded by beautiful sparkling lakes which you can live on or near–in an apartment, condo or home. Lakes Hamilton, Catherine and Ouachita surround Hot Springs and provide multiple opportunities for fishing, boating and swimming.

The area abounds in unique geological attractions. The thermal waters for which Hot Springs is famous attract many for various health reasons. The quartz crystal buried in the Ouachitas provides rockhounds and collectors with hours of enjoyment. The mountains themselves are unique. They are the only range in the Americas that run east /west, and they are the highest peaks between the Rockies and the Alleghenies.

The scenic beauty along with other factors such as housing costs, quality of life, taxes and availability of medical service have contributed to national recognition. Rand Mc Nally's <u>Retirement Places Rated</u> gave Hot Springs the high rank of #3 in the country for ideal places to retire in their 1987 and '89 editions.

Montgomery County offers many of the scenic delights of Hot Springs in a more forested, less urban setting. Thirty-five miles west of Hot Springs, Mt. Ida offers small-town living for those who might want to stretch out on acreage or simply avoid the bustle of city dwelling. It has no movies or malls and is "dry," but it is delightfully friendly and you will know most everyone.

Mt. Ida has a nursing home and the Sunset Retirement Center for ambulatory seniors. Apartment housing and rental homes are few and at a premium. However, if you choose to build, home ownership is a bargain compared to much of the United States.

Hot Springs has a wide range of retirement options. Rental units are very moderately priced. Several retirement communities exist and will fit most tastes and needs. Benedictine Manor (Second & Grand Streets) and West Shores (3207 Albert Pike, 767-1200) offer apartment living with various plans for meals or kitchen facilities. Personal care units and maid service are available. Country Club Village (3125 Malvern Road, 624-6435) offers 1200-square- foot cottages as well as apartments and is located across from Hot Springs Country Club. Hot Springs Village(1-800-228-7328) is a complete community of multi-generational living designed for the retiree of any age. Seventeen miles long by six and one-half miles wide, it has its own zipcode, four golf courses, six lakes and a fitness center. Townhouses, condos, homes and time-share units are available. Banks, groceries, and long-term care are within the boundaries of the community. The Good Samaritan Lodge is also in Hot Springs Village(#2 Cordoba Center, 501-922-2000) and features one- to three - bedroom apartment units.

The Hot Springs Chamber of Commerce has a department devoted to retirees. The development coordinator is Gail Ezelle, P.O.Box 1500,Hot Springs, AR 71902, 501-321-1878 or 1-800-326-1878. She will set up an appointment and generally help individuals with oodles of personalized information. The City of Hot Springs Retirement coordinator is Jane Anne Crone, Box K 1-800-326-1878.

Century 21

ACTION REALTY–HWY. 270
P.O. Box 540 Mt. Ida, AR 71957
(501) 867-3666 – (501) 867-2749

<u>59. Snakes</u>

Interview with Steve Goodner

Hi ,Steve. Tell me about snakes in the Ouachitas.

Your favorite kind of weather is their favorite kind. Good, beautiful fall weather is the best time. The poisonous snakes that we have here are rattlesnakes, copperheads, and down on the creeks, cottonmouths.

People crystal digging are not going to be down by the creeks. They're going to be up in the peaks.

Up in the mountains they're not going to run into a copperhead. They're certainly not going to run into a cottonmouth. But they'll run into ground rattlers–but you might run into a ground rattler anywhere. That's a pygmy rattlesnake. They're small. They can get 2-3 feet long.

Are they less deadly because of their size?

Probably. They may be less aggressive, and due to their smallness they won't hold as much venom. We have timber rattlers, and they get pretty big, maybe 5 feet or more. Diamondbacks, which you don't see too many of anymore might go over 6 feet. The diamondback is aggressive. He'll chase you; he'll stand and fight; he'll look for you.

When's the last time you saw a diamondback?
About 30 years ago.

What happens if you see a snake? What do you do?

Leave them alone. Some people are frightened of snakes, but the best thing to do is just avoid them. That's what I do. I don't kill them. There's no problem avoiding a snake, not a rattlesnake. They're not very fast. They are pretty fast to strike; I think they strike at about 8 feet per second–you can run faster than that. I've walked past copperheads and cottonmouths which did in fact strike at me and missed because I was moving.

Back to the water moccasins. What about people that are playing in the water?

Well, they are there. They don't like to be gotten real close to, and sometimes they get a little feisty. It's best to never swim alone and never put you hands or feet where you haven't first looked. Cottonmouths have a tendency to lie on low branches over the river, so it's wise to be careful when canoeing or walking.

What do you do if you see a snake swimming towards you?

I'd swim the other way. That would be the prudent thing to do. I'd get out of the water. I wouldn't mess with him. I wouldn't panic.

Your general attitude seems to be one of leaving them well enough alone and moving out of their space....

Well, they're not a particularly dangerous animal. They may be poisonous, but even if you get bitten, it's possible you're not in too much trouble. You ought to have some medical attention but don't panic. Even when people get bitten they normally don't die. The worst thing that a snake bite usually does is nerve damage in the area where you're bitten.

When you say get medical attention, should you go to a local doctor or to a hospital?
I wouldn't recommend you start jogging to go to the doctor, especially if you've had a big dose of snake venom. You need to take things as easy as you can. Yes, you need medical attention, and it helps if you can kill and take the snake with you to the hospital. This allows the doctor to administer the proper anti-venom.

Then it's probably not wise, particularly to someone new to the area, to go prowling around on these mountains alone.
I wouldn't think that it would be. There are not as many snakes as there used to be for whatever reason, but still there's a few up there. I wouldn't think anybody climbing in the rocks should be alone for lots of reasons. Snakes are not a big problem.

What kind of snakes do we have here that are not poisonous?
Lots and lots, but not as many as there used to be. We have grass snakes, chicken snakes, black snakes, coachwhips, indigo snakes, bullsnakes, rat snakes. The majority of the snakes you will find are going to be non-poisonous.

Ed.Note: Poisonous snakes have a triangular shaped head with a pointed nose and slanty eyes. They are pit vipers, so called because of the pits between their eyes and nostrils. Non-poisonous snakes have oval shaped heads with rounder noses and round eyes. If you question your ability to distinguish between the two, buy a book on the identification of snakes. In most cases moving away from the snake as quickly as possible is the best possible course of action. If bitten–go to the hospital.

60. Television

Channel 2, KETS (ETV)
Channel 4, KARK (NBC)
Channel 7, KATV (ABC)
Channel11, KTHV (CBS)

61. Wildflowers

The Hot Springs National Park has free literature on wildflowers in the area. They will also give you a calendar which notes when each species blooms and has drawings and descriptions. A checklist of Ferns and Fern Allies found in the park and surrounding Garland county is also available at the Fordyce Visitor Center.

In Mt. Ida, at the Mt. Ida Cafe, you can find <u>Primitive Medical Remedies & Natural Medicines</u> by Ray Gordon which has drawings and descriptions of local herbs growing in the area.

**To Receive Copies of Crystal Waters
Send $5.95 plus $1.05 Postage To**

**Heartland Press
H.C. 67 Box 527
Norman, AR 71960**

Substantial Discount For 10 or more Copies

Readers are encouraged to share their experiences and suggestions for future editions.Please let us know of new locations we should add. Also let us know of you experiences in the various places described in Crystal Waters!

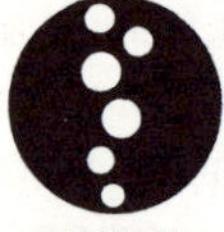

The Author

Dr. Patricia Jordan is a resident of Mt. Ida, Arkansas. She has lived in the area with her two children for three years. She is a licensed psychologist with an avocation for travel and adventure. Her experiences in the area have led her to publish this volume.

She was initially drawn to the locale by an interest in crystals and the beauty of the local surroundings. She makes her home here because of the people, the schools and the quality of life that is present.

Heartland Crystal, her shop on the Crystal Loop, will open in the fall of 1990. Weekend crystal/hot-bath retreats are available. Stop and visit on your travels.

Look for future editions of Crystal Waters. This book is the first of many updates. Please write with all comments.

MAP OF HOT SPRINGS

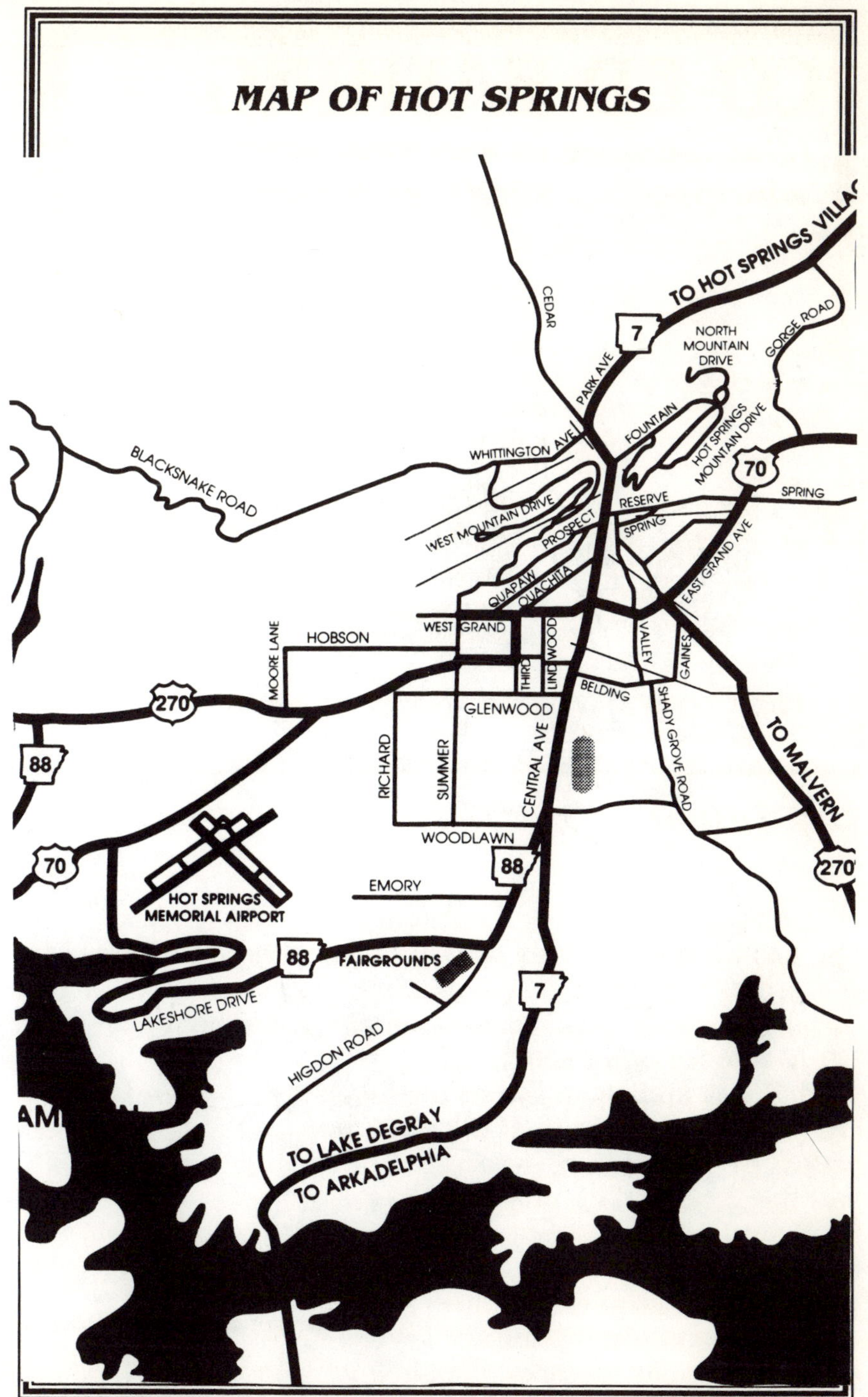

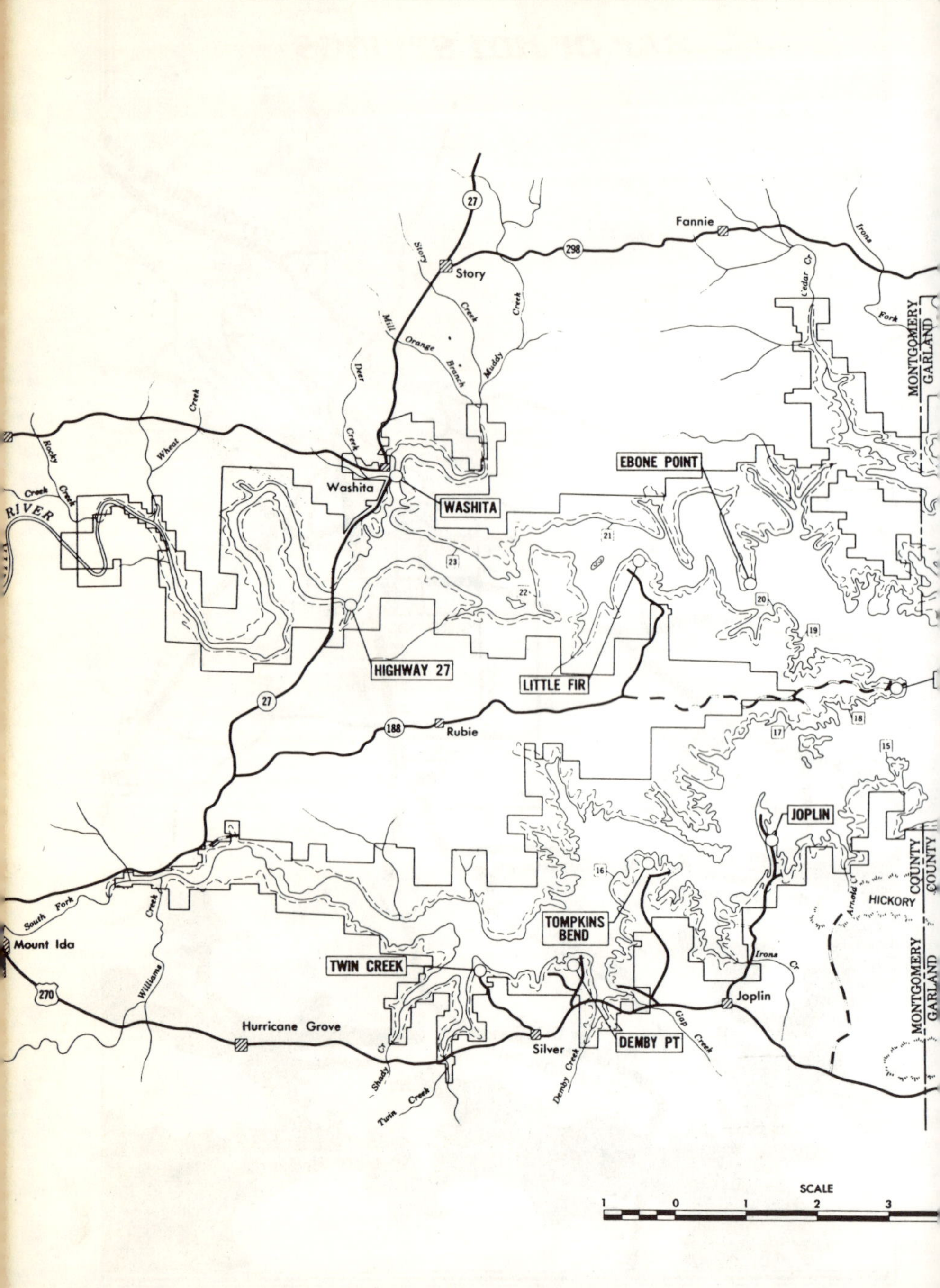
27
298
Fannie
Irons
Story
Story
Creek
Creek
Creek
Mill
Orange
Branch
Muddy
Deer
Creek
Cedar Ct
Fork
MONTGOMERY
GARLAND
Wheat
Creek
Rocky
Creek
Creek
EBONE POINT
RIVER
Washita
WASHITA
21
23
22
20
19
HIGHWAY 27
LITTLE FIR
27
188
Rubie
18
17
15
JOPLIN
Arnold Ct
HICKORY
MONTGOMERY COUNTY
GARLAND COUNTY
16
TOMPKINS
BEND
Irons Ct
South Fork
Creek
Mount Ida
TWIN CREEK
DEMBY PT
Joplin
270
Williams
Hurricane Grove
Gap Creek
Silver
MONTGOMERY
GARLAND
Ct
Shady Creek
Demby Creek
Twin Creek
SCALE
1   0   1   2   3